FROM TRAUMA TO TROPHIES

THE UNFORESEEN EVENTS THAT REDEFINED ME

Guerdy

My Memoir
GUERDY ABRAIRA

Copyright © 2025 by Guerdy Abraira

Book Cover and Back Cover Image by Jim Jordan Photography
Book Cover Design by Guerdy Abraira
Interior Design by Oseyi Okoeguale

Published by
Live Limitless Media Group

20 N Orange Ave., 11th Floor
Orlando, FL 32808
info@livelimitlessmedia.com

Author: Guerdy Abraira
Email: guerdyproductions@gmail.com
Website: www.guerdyfy.com

All rights reserved.
No part of this book may be reproduced, distributed,
or transmitted in any form or by any means, electronic or mechanical, including
photocopying, recording, or by any information storage and retrieval system,
without prior written permission from the publisher, except in the case of brief
quotations embodied in critical articles or reviews.

Live Limitless Media Group supports the right to creative
expression and the protection of intellectual property.
For permission requests,
please contact: info@livelimitlessmedia.com.

Library of Congress Cataloging-in-Publication Data

Abraira, Guerdy, author.
From Trauma to Trophies: The Unforeseen Events That Redefined Me: Guerdy Abraira.
First Edition. — Orlando, FL: Live Limitless Media Group, 2025.
Includes bibliographical references.
Identifiers:

Paperback ISBN: 978-1-952903-73-1
Hardcover ISBN: 978-1-952903-74-8

Subjects:
Autobiographical | Self-realization | Personal growth | Resilience | Entrepreneurship

Printed in the United States of America

First Edition: November 2025

DEDICATION

For my little girl
You were never born into this world, yet will always be mine.

For my Grandmere Alina,
You couldn't read or write to tell your story, so I'm writing it for both of us.
Pou ou, Grann,
Ou pa t kapab li ni ekri pou rakonte istwa ou, kidonk mwen ap ekri li pou nou toude.

To my big brother Emmanuel,
Your absence taught me presence.

To My Nieces, Kofie and Zenzie,
Gone too soon…forever loved, forever missed.

CONTENTS

> This wouldn't be a true GUERDYFY experience without bringing chapters to life.
> Scan the QR codes to explore the photos, videos, and moments that shaped my story.

Dedication iii

Foreword by Russell Abraira vi

Prologue xi

Introduction 1

PART I: Rooted in Motion

Chapter 1: Legacy in Transit 8

Chapter 2: Influence, Francaise 20

Chapter 3: The Réjouis Rules 31

Chapter 4: M.I.A. in Miami 44

Chapter 5: Learning to Belong 58

Chapter 6: Finding "My Russell" 72

Chapter 7: A Planner in the Making 86

Chapter 8: Built to Dazzle, Trained to Deliver 98

Chapter 9: My Brother, Emmanuel 106
Chapter 10: Tap Tap Tap 115
Chapter 11: The "NO" That Made Me Dangerous 120
Chapter 12: Scheduled for Collapse 130

PART II: The Journey to "ME"

Chapter 13: Paradise, Interrupted 136
Chapter 14: Boxed In 141
Chapter 15: Fighting without Armor 146
Chapter 16: The Other C-Word 150
Chapter 17: Radiating 157
Chapter 18: The Reconstruction Era 163
Chapter 19: The New Normal 171
Chapter 20: On Camera 180
Chapter 21: Let Me 187

Epilogue 195
Letter to the Nine-Year-Old Little Guerdy 200
Acknowledgements 202

FOREWORD
BY RUSSELL ABRAIRA

Not too long ago, after doing something that annoyed Guerdy, she half-jokingly asked me, as she had on different occasions before, "Who raised you!?" I reflected on our ages and quickly realized that I had a perfect opportunity to return her jab, so I responded, "You did!" She realized that I was on to something, and we both heartily laughed it off. However, this moment of reflection reminded both of us how much time flies, and that we have indeed been together for most of our lives, learning from and, in a way, shaping each other. It was thirty years ago that I decided to hug Guerdy in the hallway of North Miami Senior High, a simple action that set the trajectory of our lives in motion. From that moment on, we have been inseparable and have built our lives together filled with love, respect, and shared experiences, both good, bad, and challenging.

From the beginning, Guerdy always stood out to me. Before we ever met, I remember thinking, "she is so elegant and beautiful" but I never thought she would be into someone like me. Lo and behold, two years later she started saying hi to me in the hallway, which led to me making the move of my lifetime and giving her a huge hug which she never saw coming.

We've been through so much since that moment, and this book delves into many of the events of Guerdy's extraordinary life story.

However, I would like to touch on some of the little and not-so-little things that go unnoticed but add to the uniqueness and beauty of who my wife is. One of the greatest blessings in our life has been our two sons, who bring us joy and pride every day. They're both smart, humble, kind, and caring, and they've given us a purpose and happiness that we never imagined possible. Beyond that, I've witnessed firsthand how Guerdy has succeeded and built a name for herself as one of the top wedding planners in the world by bringing her creative visions to life for so many lucky couples.

What many forget, or simply are not aware of, is that while she was conquering the wedding planning industry, she had to embrace the role of a firefighter's wife. This role has many challenges, some obvious and some not so obvious. Guerdy has had to live with the burden and fear of me not coming home for the past twenty-five years due to the inherent risks of the job. I remember the first day I showed Guerdy the bunker gear that I would be wearing to protect me, and she immediately started to cry. At the time, I was young and didn't fully understand what the big deal was, but I fully recognize that extra, silent burden she has carried for all these years. She also had to adapt to the firefighting schedule and take care of our boys by herself for what amounts to a third of our lives. This unique but major part of our marriage essentially means that Guerdy has had two full-time jobs for twenty-five years, and she mastered both with the utmost grace and humility.

What's even more remarkable is that long before all the success and long before she became the woman the world now sees, Guerdy had already faced some of her hardest tests in life. When she was just nine years old, she and her brother were sent from Paris to Miami, separated from their parents, and left to navigate a new culture, language, and environment in an unfamiliar world. I can't imagine what that kind of emotional shock must have felt like at such a young age. Yet somehow, she managed to turn that experience into fuel. It shaped her drive, her empathy, and her need to create stability wherever she goes. I believe that the resilience she built from that experience became the foundation for everything she has accomplished since.

Over our three decades together, we've shared incredible highs and heartbreaking lows. We've traveled, grown, raised two amazing sons, and built a wonderful life brick by brick. But we've also faced challenges and tragedies that could have broken us. We endured the unimaginable loss of Guerdy's brother Emmanuel and two of his daughters during the devastating 2010 Haiti earthquake. That tragedy shook her to her core, and ever since, I've watched her carry that grief with quiet strength and grace. Then came the loss of our baby girl, which tested our ability to keep moving forward, especially given how little time had passed since losing her brother. Guerdy carried that loss with the same grace; not by rushing through it, but by allowing love to slowly lead her back to hope. In time, we were blessed with our second son, and she poured her heart into our boys, who continue to be our greatest joy and grounding force.

What people might not see, though, are the quieter layers that make Guerdy who she is. Behind the powerhouse and perfectionist, is a woman who still finds comfort in the simplest things. One of her favorite shows to watch is *Little House on the Prairie*. It's a story about family, love, and the basic joys of life. Values that truly define her. To this day, on some random weeknight before bed, she'll stream it like it just came out. I had never actually seen it myself until she made me sit down and watch it with her one evening, and now I understand why she loves it so much. It reminds her of what really matters when everything else is stripped away.

As much as she enjoys a wholesome, feel-good series like *Little House on the Prairie*, or movies like *Coming to America*, she also loves the edge and thrill of *Kill Bill* or *The Godfather*. That contrast is exactly what makes her who she is, never one-dimensional, always full of surprises.

There are also the things that make her uniquely Guerdy. She speaks four languages: Spanish, English, French, and Haitian Creole. I've always admired how she can connect with people anywhere we go. One of the funniest moments happens whenever we walk into a Latin restaurant. Oftentimes, people immediately start speaking to me in Spanish while ignoring her. I just point to Guerdy and say, "You're talking to the wrong one." You can see the surprise turn into admiration. It's a small thing, but it sums her up perfectly, always full of surprises and impossible to box in.

What's interesting is that for someone who can connect with so many different kinds of people in any setting, there are still times when she finds herself out of rhythm. Guerdy has a presence that is commanding, but not because she tries to be. She leads with her heart and genuine enthusiasm, and sometimes that level of openness catches people off guard. For example, when she greets someone with her full energy by smiling, complimenting, and instantly lifting the mood, some don't know how to receive it. They mistake her exuberance for something performative, when in reality, it's just who she is. The truth is, everything she does comes from the right place. Her kindness and loyalty run deep, and her intentions are always rooted in care. I've seen how she gives so much of herself to people, even when they don't always meet her with the same heart. She always says that next time she won't overextend herself, but she just can't help it. That's who she is. She's been burned many times, but she never lets that change who she is. I've been proud to watch her evolve and finally stand up for herself. She may seem tough and unshakable, but underneath that strength, she's soft and deeply sensitive. I'm glad she's learning not to let people mistake her kindness for weakness, as she often says. Every time I think I know every side of her, she grows again, becoming an even more layered version of herself. She likes to joke that I'm traumatized from living through all her highs and lows, but the truth is, I'm amazed. I'm proud. And every time I see her rise, I say to myself, that's my wife. Resilience isn't something she learned; it's something she is.

That strength would soon be tested again through a new chapter neither of us saw coming: cancer. I still remember the day we found out. I stayed calm for her, but inside I was terrified. I've spent my entire adult life aiding people in danger, yet nothing prepared me for watching the person I love most have to face something I couldn't fix. From that moment on, my role shifted from protector to supporter, and I learned that sometimes strength means simply standing beside someone as they fight their own battle.

I've seen every version of my wife: the dreamer, the doer, the mother, the survivor, and more. And as someone who's been by her side since nearly the beginning, I can say with absolute certainty that *this book, From Trauma to Trophies,* isn't just a memoir; it's proof that every setback becomes her spark, and like a phoenix, she rises from it with even more fire.

—Russell Abraira

HIGH SCHOOL PROM 1996

WEDDING 2002
PHOTO CREDIT: FRANK PANARO

DATE NIGHT 2025
PHOTO CREDIT: GIANO CURRIE

PROLOGUE

The groom said no. Right there at the altar, beneath the sweeping branches of a majestic banyan tree. My hand was instantly on my walkie-talkie as the words left his mouth, already moving to contain the moment.

"Time stamp: 5:42 PM." I logged it in my head like courtroom evidence because I knew this was the kind of moment that would echo far beyond that tree.

I lowered my voice, steady but firm, issuing commands through my walkie-talkie to the entire team.

PHOTO BY JONATHAN SCOTT

"Remove all monograms immediately." The cake had to go, along with the party favors, napkins, menus, and pillows. Every trace of initials erased. I told the caterer to start pouring drinks and passing hors d'oeuvres without delay, creating an illusion of celebration in a space that was anything but. On my command, the energy shifted. No chaos. No meltdown. Just controlled redirection.

I even called security, though I'm not sure why. Maybe it was just to reassure myself that I was still in control. Control had always been the point. It's why I chose this profession in the first place.

I was the fixer. Always. I absorbed the stress so no one else had to. It was my superpower, until the day it left me powerless. Because I usually saw everything coming.

Except those four words: "You have breast cancer."

INTRODUCTION

BECOMING HER

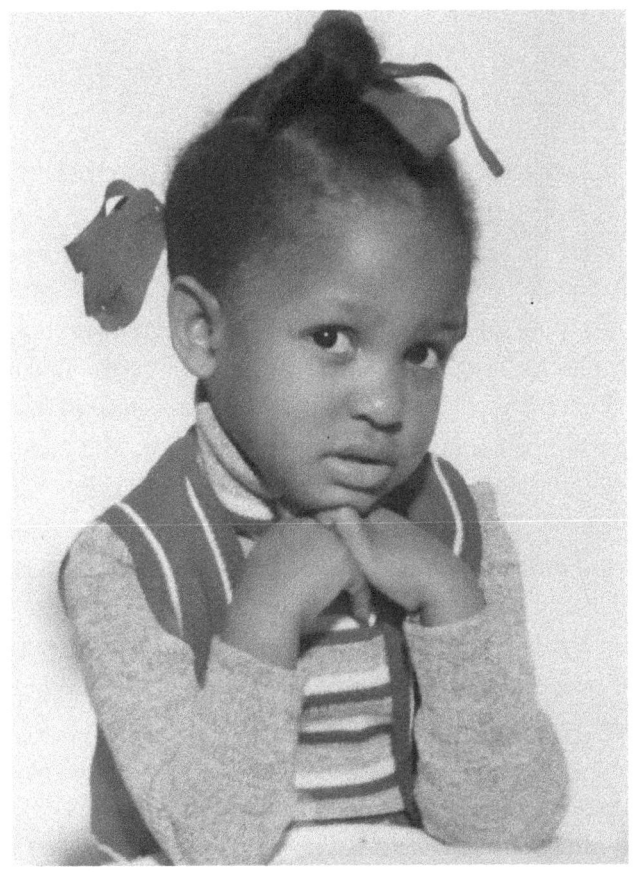

GUERDY AT AGE 3

PHOTO CREDIT: JIM JORDAN PHOTOGRAPHY 2024

We were lost. Lost in the most helpless way, sitting on the cold tile floor of an unfamiliar lobby. My grandmother, Alina, couldn't read or write, and I was too young to help her find our way back. I remember her holding me and her purse closely, waiting for someone to open a door or recognize her face. We had not just gotten lost that day. In many ways, we were still trying to find our way, even though it had already been a couple of years since we arrived in France. I was under two years old when my parents left Haiti for Paris, hoping for a better life.

Paris was supposed to be a place of new beginnings, but settling into our new hometown wasn't easy. We finally secured our own apartment in Meudon-La-Forêt, a quiet suburb just outside the city lined with uniform buildings and narrow streets that all seemed to blend together. It wasn't glamorous, but it was ours, a small sign of stability after so much change. The apartment was located inside a development of buildings that all looked identical, with the same facades, the same doorways, the same trimmings, and very little signage to tell them apart. To my grandmother, the buildings all looked alike, almost impossible to tell apart.

One afternoon, Grandma Alina decided to take me out with her to gather groceries. My father had given her precise instructions to help her navigate her way to the market and back home. He told her which landmarks to notice, which doors to enter, and which direction to turn so she could find her way back. She had practiced with him a few times and felt ready. Although my grandmother was illiterate, she was resourceful and had always relied on her sharp memory and instincts to navigate the world. That day, however, when we tried to return home, everything blurred together. The landmarks were indistinguishable, the buildings mirrored one another, and she couldn't tell which apartment was ours.

In a desperate attempt to find our way, we circled one building, then another, then another, until the reality set in that we were lost. Years later, I asked my grandmother about that day, and she admitted she hadn't wanted me to see her panic. But even then, as a little girl, I felt her unease. Her sighs grew heavier as she studied each building, hoping one would look familiar. Her intensity deepened when none of them did. I remember holding tightly to my grandmother's hand, the one missing two fingers, as she retraced her steps frantically yet gracefully, managing her fear step by step, loop after loop, until she was too tired and overwhelmed to keep trying.

When someone opened the door to a nearby building, she led me inside to wait. There were no cell phones back then, so she couldn't call anyone. Inside the building, there were no chairs, only the cold tile floor. She sat down with me in her lap and gave me a piece of candy from her pocket, another loving attempt to maintain calm in what must have felt like chaos. She always carried candy for me in her purse, and in that moment it gave me a sense of protection and normalcy. I remember watching her clutch her purse tightly, her grip strong and unrelenting, as if it were the last bit of dignity she had left.

She was unable to ask for help from the people passing by. Everyone seemed caught up in their own version of survival. Some glanced our way and kept moving because stillness was a luxury none of them could afford. It felt like everyone was trying to keep their own balance in a world that didn't stop moving, and we were the only ones sitting still. As a little girl, that day etched itself into me as a core memory. It wasn't just about being lost. It was about being unseen.

Eventually my father found us. It was nearly nightfall when he spotted us. He had searched building by building until he finally found my grandmother and me sitting on the floor. You could see the relief on his face. He didn't scold my grandmother or question how she could've gotten lost. He simply brought us home. I never forgot that day; the ache in my legs, the hunger in my stomach, the chill of the floor against my skin. That lobby became the setting for my first real memory of powerlessness. Somewhere in that silence, something shifted in me. Never again, I thought. Never again would I sit hopeless and helpless, waiting to be rescued. Even though we had been found safe and unharmed, the helplessness of that day stayed with me. It was in that waiting, in that uncertainty, that I began to build self-reliance. I carried it with me into how I studied, how I competed, how I executed, and how I showed up in the world. Self-reliance became not only how I functioned but my default setting and the foundation for my pursuit of excellence in all things.

My childhood was marked by constant motion. I was always adapting or starting over. By the time I was nine, I had already lived in three countries on two different continents. With all the shifts my family and I maneuvered, my parents maintained and asserted their high expectations of my siblings and me. In my family, the Réjouis Rules were simple: excellence was expected. So I did what I was taught. I excelled. I always worked to be faster, better, stronger. The problem was, I was in a constant race with no finish line. What began as obedience to my parents' expectations became my identity. My worth came from what I could do and how well I could deliver. I believed that if I could just do enough and achieve enough, then I would be enough.

For years, that mindset seemed to work. People saw the success: the magazine covers, the television show, the thriving businesses, the marriage, the children, the glamorous events. It was all real. I built it. I earned it. But momentum became my coping mechanism. I thought that if I kept moving, I was winning. Then, one day, life forced me to stop.

It forced me to face the parts of myself I had always placed last: my traumas, my triggers, my body, my healing, my truth. It made me question everything I had ever called success. It made me face the mirror and ask myself what happens when the woman who shows up for everyone else finally has to show up for herself. That question became the starting point for this book.

I wrote this book for anyone who has ever dreamed of having it all. But before you turn the page expecting a manual on how to achieve that goal, let me be clear: this is not a guide about trophies, success, or perfection. It is a story about what those things really mean once you have them and what they cannot give you in return. It is also about the trauma behind the trophies, the lessons behind the victories, and the peace that can come only after the noise fades.

The first half of this book, Part I: *Rooted in Motion*, is about that climb. I went from being a little girl lost in a lobby and limited by language barriers, to building a life that some would say is beyond imagination. Yet every piece of it was built with intention. The second half, Part II: *The Journey to Me*, is about what happens when life interrupts that performance. My interruption came in the form of personal losses and reflection. Yours may be something else; maybe heartbreak, betrayal, illness, or failure. This part of my story is about learning to pause, self-reflect, and to allow those experiences to reshape you into the newest version of yourself. It is about doing the work to grow, and once you do that work, realizing that your growth becomes too great to return to who you used to be. It is realizing that life is not about proving your worth but resting in it.

From Trauma to Trophies is where my motion met meaning and where the roots that once held me down began leading me home. In that surrender, I stepped into the truest version of myself, Guerdy 2.0. But I'm not ready to tell you about her just yet. To understand who I am now, you need to understand who I was then. Let me take you back to the beginning.

PART I
ROOTED IN MOTION

MY PARENTS' WEDDING DAY, HAITI, 1970

Chapter 1
LEGACY IN TRANSIT

My full name is Guerdy Elischéba Réjouis. But from birth, the name I went by wasn't Guerdy, it was my middle name, Elischéba. Pronounced Eh-lee shay-bah. Réjouis is pronounced Ray-zjwee. There's a story behind why I switched it to Guerdy which I'll share later when I talk about my move to Miami. Growing up, my nickname was Babette. Elischéba is a biblical name, inspired by Queen Sheba, a powerful woman known for her wisdom, beauty, and boldness. I was born in Port-au-Prince, Haiti, at 4:00 a.m. on January 4, 1978. I am told I stood out from the start, being the only girl born that morning among a room full of newborn boys. The doctor took one look at me and told my mother, "This one is going to be very special in this world."

I was born into chaos. Haiti was growing more and more unstable under the tightening grip of the Duvalier dictatorship. While I don't remember any of it, my birth sits at the center of a pivotal shift in my family's legacy: from being planted in Haiti to being uprooted for good. I would later come to understand just how many forces were already in motion the morning I came into this world. There's a French phrase I love: *mise en mouvement*, which means "put into motion." That's what my birth felt like in retrospect. It was the start of a life that would never stop moving.

Before it was called Haiti, it was Ayiti, the land of high mountains. The original name given by the Indigenous Taíno people. Then came colonization. The Spanish renamed the island Hispaniola, and eventually the French took control of the western side and called it Saint-Domingue. The name Haiti was not simply a rebrand. It was a resurrection. A reclaiming.

In 1804, Haiti became the first Black republic to win its independence after defeating the French in the only successful slave revolt in modern history. A nation born in resistance, but the price of that victory was devastating. France demanded reparations for their "loss of property", and by "property," they meant enslaved human beings. Haiti had to pay the equivalent of billions of dollars over generations, just to be left alone. The rest of the world joined in punishing Haiti by isolating it politically and economically. Our revolution terrified them. It made clear what enslaved and colonized people were capable of, and they never forgave us for that.

My father was born in Haiti during a time when the country was still trying to stand upright under the weight of those consequences. By the time he was a grown man, Haiti was trapped in a dictatorship under François "Papa Doc" Duvalier. When Papa Doc died in 1971, his son Jean-Claude "Baby Doc" took over, continuing his father's brutal regime. It was a time of deep fear and repression.

Haiti's most terrifying weapon wasn't even its government, it was the Tonton Macoutes. A paramilitary force loyal only to the president. They wore dark sunglasses, carried machetes, and operated completely outside the law. There was no protection, no warning, no logic. You could vanish in the middle of the day for something you said and sometimes, for no reason at all. Disappearances, torture, and public beatings were normal. People were dragged off to the most feared place in Haiti: Fort Dimanche. It was called a prison, but it wasn't just a prison. It was a death sentence. Located near La Saline in Port-au-Prince, it became infamous under François "Papa Doc" Duvalier. Declared a historical monument in 1987, it remains a chilling reminder of what unchecked power can do.

The Tonton Macoutes weren't professional officers. Most were poor, uneducated men pulled in for their blind loyalty to Duvalier. Some were chosen based on rumors of voodoo ties, others simply because they would obey without question. The regime rewarded them with unchecked power. As long as they kept the population scared, they could do whatever they wanted. The sunglasses they wore weren't just a disguise, they made them less human, more shadow than man.

No one felt safe, not even my father's younger cousins. One day, without warning or explanation, two of his three cousins were taken away. They had promising futures, but in a country where hope itself could be mistaken for rebellion, that did not matter. They were never seen again. The third cousin narrowly escaped, and although I will share the full story later, that single act of survival quietly set everything into motion for our family.

And so, my story, before I ever took a breath, was already being shaped by political terror and impossible choices. Haiti wasn't just our homeland. It was our battleground, and my father, like so many others, made the heartbreaking decision to leave behind everything familiar to protect what mattered most: his family's future.

Though I looked like my dad in the face, I'm told that parts of my personality traits were that of my maternal great-grandmother,

Roxanne Louissant. She was my Grandma Alina's mother. And from everything I've heard, she was not the kind of woman you forgot. Roxanne was the definition of no-nonsense. She smoked a pipe, rode on a donkey and carried herself like a woman who didn't need or ask for help. She kicked out her husband, Sean, after catching him cheating on her while she was pregnant with my Grandma Alina. Instead of folding, she raised her children alone. She worked, survived, and she did what needed to be done.

I never met Roxanne unfortunately, but I'm told that I carry her spirit. It wasn't common for a woman to ride a donkey alone down dirt roads, but Roxanne wasn't a common woman. She got on, held her head high, and moved forward, because that's what life demanded.. The same way she made do with what she had, I learned how to build with what I was given. She wasn't the kind of woman who waited for permission. Neither am I. That unyielding need to take charge, to push forward, to figure it out on your own, that's not something I learned. That's something I inherited. We were built to endure, especially Grandma Alina.

When Grandma Alina was a baby, something traumatic happened to her. Roxanne, her mom, overwhelmed and exhausted one afternoon, fell asleep while smoking her pipe and holding Alina in her arms. In that haze, the lit pipe came into contact with the baby's delicate hand, and two of my grandmother's index fingers were burned so badly they had to be amputated. I can only imagine the horror of that moment; the guilt Roxanne must have carried; and the emotional scars my grandmother bore, even if she didn't consciously remember it. The aftermath followed my grandmother throughout her life. She was small in stature, reserved in spirit, with a confidence that never seemed to blossom fully. You could feel the shadow from her past, but you could also feel her grit. A woman of few words. She was illiterate, as I mentioned before, yet she did just fine without these skillsets. Her language was devotion. Her loyalty was unshakable. Her hands were always busy and her mind always alert.

Where Roxanne, her mother, was fire, Grandma Alina was stone; quiet, steady, unmoving. She wasn't outwardly affectionate in the traditional sense. There were no bedtime stories or over-the-top declarations of love. But her love was always there. It was demonstrated in the way she sliced fruit with care, in the way she sat beside me without saying a word, and in the way she carried the weight of the household without ever needing to be thanked. She had cataracts in both eyes, and also a condition called arcus semilis, which gave her pupils a pale blue sheen. And though she could not see clearly, she saw everything. She was the most significant person in my life; more so than my mother in many ways. My grandmother was always there. Always physically present yet comfortable in the background, and never needing the spotlight. She anchored me. She was my constant.

She didn't laugh loudly. She didn't gossip. She wasn't flashy. She didn't even try to adapt to the "French" customs when we moved there. She remained fully Haitian, and fully herself, which I now realize was its own quiet rebellion. She refused to be diluted. And for me, that was powerful. She showed me that identity isn't something you beg to keep, it's something you quietly refuse to let go of. When I think about the women who shaped me, it's not just their story. It's a lineage. My great-grandmother Roxanne gave me my backbone, my grandma Alina gave me my grounding, and her daughter, my mother, gave me my wit. Together, their legacy lives in everything I've become.

Alina had to go straight to work at a young age to help support her family. Life didn't offer her another kind of path. But books couldn't teach what she knew. Her wisdom came from living. From surviving. She had this strength in her silence, this power in her presence. She taught without knowing she did, loved without needing praise, and held space like it was sacred.

Alina's father, Sean Sena, was born in Camagüey, Cuba. My love of salsa, my ear for Latin rhythm, and the way I move when that beat drops; it was never a question; it never needed explanation. It's in the blood, and it always showed. Sean was born to Antonio Sena, a Cuban native, and Clémence Clermont, a Haitian woman who had arrived in Cuba as a child with her parents. That detail, Clémence's childhood migration, anchors our story in the wider history between Haiti and Cuba. Following the Haitian Revolution of 1804, which made Haiti the first free Black republic in the world, French colonizers fled the island in fear. While we don't know for certain why the Clermont family left Haiti for Cuba, history suggests they may have been taken there during the exodus of French colonizers. Whether by force or through circumstances beyond their control, we may never know. But what's clear is that their journey was shaped by the ripple effects of revolution. Today, Creole is the second most spoken language in Cuba, and more than 300,000 people of Haitian descent live on the island.

Sean grew up in Cuba, raised with his two siblings, Julio and Antonia, in a household that leaned heavily into Cuban culture. They spent their formative years on the island until Sean turned sixteen, when his family returned to Haiti. There, Sean met and married Roxanne at Cathédrale St. Marc. They had six children, Alina (my grandmother), Aurélia, Loreda, Fernando, Andrea, and Marcia. Despite their Haitian lineage, they were given Spanish names. It was a quiet act of cultural blending, one of many woven throughout our family history.

Grandma Alina married my grandfather, Metaus Désir, in 1945. They lived on the island of La Gonâve, the largest island in Haiti. Historically, La Gonâve was a place of refuge. During the colonial period, it remained largely untouched by colonizers, which made it a sanctuary for the Taíno people fleeing early Spanish violence. Later, runaway slaves also sought safety there, escaping the brutality of the French plantation system on the mainland. Even in modern times, it has remained relatively remote, with about 85,000 residents relying on fishing, subsistence farming, and trade with the mainland. My grandfather sold watermelons from a boat and farmed the land, while my grandmother ran a small variety goods shop. Together they had five kids with my mom being the oldest. Of all the kids, my mom, Emilie, was the only one to be sent away for studies. She had started speaking at an unusually very early age, and her scholastic potential was recognized from the very beginning. Everyone who came in contact with her praised and recognized her witty ways and mature grasp for learning. It was undeniable and her parents had to make a difficult decision. It was very common back then, in Haiti, for children to go live with relatives who lived in cities and places where there were more opportunities available, so they decided to send her to live with Grandma Alina's older sister. There, she would be closer to Port-au-Prince for a proper Catholic Boarding School education.

Her earliest schooling was under the supervision of Madame Jacqueline Turian Cordozo, a trailblazer in early childhood education. Jacqueline was the daughter of Maud Hudicourt Turian Devarieux, a prominent Haitian educator who had run a reputable school and boarding house on Chemin des Dalles during the 1930s and 1940s. This institution served families from the provincial bourgeoisie who wanted their children educated in the capital.

When Jacqueline returned from Europe in the late 1940s, she brought with her new ideas about early childhood learning that emphasized creativity and hands-on experiences. Instead of strict memorization or heavy discipline, her classrooms encouraged children to explore, imagine, and learn through activities that felt more like games than lessons. She opened Haiti's first school of its kind inside her mother's education center. Later, she moved the school to Impasse Lavaud, where it became one of the most respected early learning programs in the country. It was in this environment, nurtured by the hands of women who dared to evolve tradition, that my mother began her education. And just like the women before her, she stepped into the unknown bravely, not by chance, but by lineage. She continued on to boarding school at *Lécole Notre-Dame-du-Perpetuel-Secours (Les Filles de Marie), a catholic school and then went off to Cœur Immaculé de Marie.* Education shaped her, but so did faith.

Grandpa Metaus, my mother's father, fell ill suddenly and passed away from colon cancer on February 20, 1969. It was a devastating blow for the family. My grandmother, never one to show emotion, swallowed her sorrow and kept going. She continued running her small commerce shop while raising her four remaining children. Eventually, the weight became too much, and she made the difficult decision to send them to live with relatives while she figured out how to survive long-term. My mother was already 18 by then. She had completed her schooling and was actively looking for a teaching job.

My parents met in October 1969. Some might call it coincidence, but to me, it feels more like destiny. My father, then 24, had just graduated with a theology degree from Nazarene Theological Seminary in Pétion-Ville that April. He was also an avid volleyball player. One day, he went to play with some friends at a school gym. My mother happened to be at that same school that day, applying and interviewing for a teaching position at the school. She was in the principal's office when my father came in briefly to ask the principal a question. Their eyes met, just once, but it was enough.

By chance, they both left the building around the same time and boarded the same bus. Normally reserved and quiet, much like my husband, both Scorpios; my father did something uncharacteristic. He gathered the courage to speak to her. Her beauty had pulled him in. He couldn't resist.

They clicked quickly. But almost just as quickly, they discovered something that could have been a major obstacle. He was Protestant and she was Catholic. And in Haiti, especially at that time, that difference wasn't a small one. There was a real tension between those two worlds.

My father, Louis, had been raised in the mountains of Haiti, in the commune of Léogâne. That land holds deep historical weight. Léogâne was once Yaguana, the birthplace of Anacaona, the Taíno queen who ruled Xaragua, the last independent Taíno kingdom on the island. She resisted colonization until she was executed by the Spanish in the early 1500s. Her legacy still lives in that soil.

My father came from that soil. His family carried Taíno blood. You could see it in their features. That lineage gave them a certain strength of spirit. He left the mountains to pursue his education in theology and ultimately became a pastor, a title that carried real weight in our culture. His own father had passed away young, as had many of his siblings, so he had to grow up fast and take responsibility early.

When my mother married my father on Saturday, May 9th, 1970, at Église de Nazaréen on Rue Dr. Aubry in Port-au-Prince, she converted to Protestantism. But old habits die hard, she would still quietly pray with her rosary and perform Catholic rituals behind closed doors before fully committing to her new faith.

They called each other nicknames, "Milou" for my mother, Emilie, and "Loulou" for my father, Louis. It was the kind of love that fostered unity and legacy, and needless to say, children came quickly. Emmanuel arrived first, followed by my oldest sister, then the twins, my other brother, and me. By the time I was born in 1978, there were already six of us. My younger sister would come later, born in France. We were a family blooming in the thick of their love. A love bubble culminated through six kids in eight years. Raising a family requires a village, especially a family of 8. My mother worked very hard for her family, but she needed help, so Grandma Alina came to stay. She moved with us to France, and later to Miami. Of all the girls, I was the one who looked the most like my father. I had the same bubbly cheeks and the same dimpled chin. My younger sister also resembled him, but not like I did. I was his reflection. I was also the only one who took up volleyball like he did. The others played tennis, soccer, and ran track.

Their love story, like so many others in our family, was soon tested by the political climate. So, here's the full story of the three cousins I mentioned earlier. They ran a barbershop together. One day, Tonton Macoute raided the shop without any warning. Two of them were taken straight to Fort Dimanche and never returned. The third cousin, Yvan, wasn't there during the raid. When he heard what had happened to his brothers, he knew they would be looking for him next. Desperate to disappear, his mother came up with a plan to disguise him in women's clothing, not just to flee the hot zone, but to flee Haiti altogether. Working quietly through friends and contacts abroad, they were able to get him safely out of the country and into France. It would be his escape that became the turning point for our family.

The regime was coming for anyone connected to the family. To this day, we still don't know why they were targeted or what exactly triggered the raid. But we knew the outcome could be fatal. By that time, my father was deeply involved in the church. Being a Protestant pastor in Haiti made you visible in a dangerous way. The Duvalier regime didn't like anyone who made people think too much, especially about justice, peace, or fairness. The Catholic Church had more protection. My father wasn't political, there was no agenda in his sermons. He simply preached kindness, dignity, and human value. But even messages like that were viewed as threatening. By contrast, a Catholic priest named Jean-Bertrand Aristide was becoming a public figure during that time, openly speaking about injustice and advocating for the poor. He would eventually go on to become president. But unlike Aristide, my father wasn't trying to build a movement. He wasn't stirring crowds or seeking attention. He was just a man of faith, quietly serving his congregation in a country where even that could be dangerous. My father realized it wasn't safe for us to stay. He knew that being a man of faith wouldn't shield him. On the contrary, It put a target on his back. That's when he made the decision that changed the trajectory of our family. We had to leave Haiti.

When my father recounts this story, he always mentions the dream. Months before the raid, he had a random vivid vision of an Air France plane in the sky. At the time, it made no sense. But when his cousins were raided, he knew it had been a sign preparing him for what was to come. So, with a heavy heart, he left for France, alone, to prepare properly for the rest of us to join him.

When he landed in Paris, he was dropped off at a motel where another Haitian refugee had been staying. Yvan had connected him with a French missionary named Roger, who helped him get his bearings. Back then, seeking political asylum wasn't as simple as just saying you felt unsafe. It required sacrifice, proof, and declaration. For my father, the price to pay for refuge was painful, he had to officially denounce Haiti and swear he wouldn't return. As a man of principle and a pastor who loved his community and congregation, this was a soul-wrenching decision, but it was one he made for the survival and wellbeing of our family. . Staying in Haiti meant danger and returning could mean death.

In order to secure our futures, my father did what was necessary and he swore never to return to our beloved island. . It was a painful oath, but it was protection. Within a few months, he sent for the rest of us, leaving behind the only home we had ever known. Even though we were moving to a foreign land, we weren't lost, it felt more like we were being carried to a new place with fresh opportunities and no threats to our lives. From my great grandmother Roxanne's strength, to my grandmother Alina's resolve; From the hills of Léogâne to the churches of Port-au-Prince, from the terror of a life-altering raid to the hope carried by a flight to freedom, life was always in motion. Our bloodline went from Haiti to Cuba, then back to Haiti; from Haiti to France, and from France to Miami. Uprooted, yes. But never unanchored. What moved with us through fear, faith, and fortitude was our legacy in transit.

THE RÉJOUIS FAMILY, (GUERDY IN FATHER'S ARMS), HAITI, 1978

Chapter 2

INFLUENCE, FRANCAISE

French life for us truly began in Meudon-La-Forêt, in that same apartment complex where Grandma and I had once been lost. The buildings all looked the same, but within those walls, life slowly began to feel familiar. With the help of nonprofit foundations and missionary organizations dedicated to supporting migrating families, we transitioned quickly. They connected my parents with essential resources, job opportunities and support systems that made it easier for us to integrate into the community.

My father, grounded in his theology degree and fluent in both French and Creole, was able to secure a position within the local religious community. He was a man of deep faith and quiet charm, which translated easily across borders. My mother went right to work too. She was not domesticated since she had spent most of her years in Haiti studying. My mother and her mom, Grandma Alina made quite the pair as my grandma would hold it down domestically while my mother was great at clerical tasks. She effortlessly completed all the necessary paperwork for us kids to be officially registered in the French government system as well as registering us for school etc. I can only imagine how overwhelming it all had to be for my mother, but she thrived in this type of setting. I definitely inherited her tenacious, "never take no" attitude. She was relentless and ambitious, fitting in seamlessly with the grit of France.

While my parents were out hustling to get us settled in, Grandma Alina was our anchor, our constant, our soft place to land. She was my favorite person in the house and I was her favorite of us kids. Maybe because I was the youngest, so she, by default, spent more time with me than the others. I think it may have quietly bothered my mom, but that was just the way it was. Plus, we had been through something together, she and I. That moment in the lobby in France, sitting in the corner in absolute silence for hours, the two of us waiting for hope to come. It etched a forever bond between us. She was mine and I was hers. She was a loving yet unemotional person. She always seemed grumpy while doing household chores, especially laundry. I remember the times when she would mumble to herself. She did it so often that it became normal background noise for us. She had this very Haitian little habit of "tchwipe" with her mouth. It's a teeth-sucking way of showing disapproval; a quick sound you make by pulling your teeth against your lips. No words, just that sharp noise, and everyone knew exactly what it meant. Haitians use it when something doesn't add up, when kids are acting up, or when they want to make their point without saying a thing. One tchwipe could do the work of a whole lecture. For us kids, it became part of the rhythm of home. Alina could swipe at us one second, and then, the moment her eyes met ours, her whole face would break into a smile. That was her balance, discipline on one side, love on the other. She didn't pretend and she didn't perform. She simply was.

There were lots of kids living in and around our apartment complex so staying entertained was never an issue. Our neighborhood was like a little crossroads of the world and was full of diverse families who had come from all over. Everyone there was trying to build a better life. Haitians, Moroccans, Algerians, and Africans lived side by side in the same apartment complex. Nobody had everything, but everybody had something, and together it worked. Everyone supported each other in small ways like buying food and goods from each other's shops. The Algerians made and sold hot and spicy merguez, the kind of sausage you couldn't forget once you tasted it. The Africans braided our hair. I can still remember sitting for hours on a low stool; the sting on my scalp as they pulled the braids tight; their fingers quick and sure, almost too fast to follow. It hurt, but it also made us girls feel beautiful, and there was a sense of pride in walking out with fresh braids that everyone in the neighborhood recognized.

The courtyard was filled with the aromas of different kitchens. You could smell stews heavy with spices, grilled meats, fried plantains, and fresh bread all mingling together in the air. Even if you didn't eat at someone's table, you shared in their life through the scents that drifted from their windows.

For us kids, the apartment complex itself was our playground. We didn't need much. We played hopscotch with chalk lines drawn on the pavement, we jumped rope until the rope burned our ankles, and we played tag until we collapsed on the pavement, sweaty and laughing. The courtyard was alive with children's laughter, rising above all those different accents and backgrounds.

Looking back, I see how much we all had in common. We were all there for the same reason; to survive, to build, and to dare to design the lives we dreamed of. France wasn't perfect, but it was a place where you had a fighting chance.

We might have spoken different languages and cooked different foods, but we were tied together by the same hope. Those first few years felt like home. Our apartment may have been modest, but it was full of structure, laughter, and Haitian warmth. We had only three bedrooms and were a family of nine; my parents, six of us kids plus Grandma Alina; yet it was perfect. This was us.

Paris itself had a magic you couldn't miss. People called it the City of Love, and even as kids we felt its charm. Cobblestone streets lined with patisseries and boutiques invited us to wander. Sometimes we went out just to window shop, taking in all the wanderlust sights. French women were a vision: so elegant and stylish with their silk scarves tied neatly, red stained lips, coats tailored to perfection, and always moving with an air of ease. Their aesthetic wasn't about wealth. It was about taste, refinement and presence. .

In France, meals weren't something to hurry through, they were a ritual. It wasn't only about feeding yourself, but more so a reminder to slow down, notice details, and savor each thing on its own. At first it felt strange, but over time it became normal. Every meal had a rhythm. First there were starters like a small salad, soup, or plate of charcuterie with slices of ham and saucisson. Then came the main dish, usually with meat, fish, or chicken, served with vegetables and potatoes. There was always bread on the table; usually a baguette, cut into slices or hand-ripped and passed around. And after the main dish, the French didn't rush to dessert like Americans. Instead, they brought out cheese. A board with different kinds; some soft and creamy, some hard and sharp, some that smelled so strong that they filled the room before you even tasted them. At first, we didn't know what to do with cheese, because in Haiti it wasn't part of our meals at all. That was a new world for us.

Then, only after the cheese, came dessert. Sometimes it was fruit; sometimes a tarte; sometimes custard or chocolate mousse. And even then, the meal wasn't over. People lingered at the table sipping wine while in deep intellectual conversation long after all the food was gone. That was the French way. The table wasn't just about eating, it was about being together, enjoying the company of friends and family, and basking in the ambiance of the moment

Haitian food was different, with bolder flavors and rich aromas. Rice and beans were always the foundation. Sometimes white rice with sauce pwa (a smooth bean purée made from black or red beans, or pigeon peas), poured over the top. Other times it was diri kole, where the red beans were cooked right into the rice, giving every grain a reddish-brown color and a rich, earthy taste. These were the staples my parents had always known, and they became the ones I learned to love too.

My favorite Haitian dish was, and still is, legim. Legim is a vegetable stew with carrots, cabbage, eggplant, chayote, spinach, and watercress, all seasoned with epis; the Haitian seasoning base of garlic, onions, peppers, thyme, and parsley. It is all slowly cooked down until the vegetables soften into a thick, flavorful casserole. Some families added meat like beef, crab, or even oxtail, but I always liked my legim with mostly just vegetables. For me, meat was an optional choice. Served over diri kole, it was hearty, comforting, and felt like home.

There were plenty of other dishes too. Poul nan sòs, chicken stewed in a tomato-based sauce. Griot; fried pork, made crispy on the outside and tender inside, and always served with pikliz, the spicy pickled cabbage and carrots that lit your mouth on fire. Bannann peze; twice-fried plantains, salted and golden, the kind you couldn't stop eating. And soup joumou; the pumpkin soup Haitians eat every New Year's Day, made with beef, vegetables, pasta, and seasoned broth. That dish wasn't just food, it was history; a tradition born from the day Haiti won its independence in 1804, and a yearly reminder of resilience and freedom.

Haitian meals didn't come in courses like French ones. Everything was served on one plate, bold and generous; each flavor standing strong but blending into the others. Where French meals were drawn out, with pauses and ceremony; Haitian meals came all at once, lively and filling. Haiti gave me food with soul but France taught me to savor. Together they shaped my taste, and taught me that food is memory, identity, and culture all in one.

At home, music was constant. My mom loved her records. Nana Mouskouri and Mireille Mathieu were the queens of our living room. I used to flip through their album covers, staring at Nana's ever-changing hairstyles and big glasses, and Mireille with her signature bowl cut hairdo. For my mom, they weren't just singers. They were guides. They represented a type of 'Girl Power' movement. She had six kids in eight years, and I can't imagine how overwhelming it must have been, trying to raise a family, stay afloat, and still feel like herself. Those albums gave her a way to feel cool, connected, even glamorous. They reminded her that she was still a young woman, not just a mother. Watching her, I saw how those songs helped her build confidence in her style, in her presence and in the way she carried herself. She believed in the idea that you should dress how you want to be addressed, and she lived by it.

We listened to all music genres at home. The 80s were alive with songs that defined the decade. Dorothée was huge back then; she even had her own children's program on the French television channel, TF1, that every kid seemed to watch. We were glued to it; obsessed with her songs that played straight from the TV into our living room. Singing along to Dorothée was part of how we learned French, repeating every lyric until it stuck.

"Hou la menteuse" "liar, liar" was about a girl whose brother kept teasing her about being in love. We thought it was hilarious and copied it at home. One of us would pop out from behind a door and start singing "Hou la menteuse, elle est amoureuse!" just to bug another sibling. It became our own running joke and a way to get under each other's skin. And getting that song right; every word and every tease, made us feel cool. Like we were finally keeping up with the French kids around us.

It was also the very first record our parents ever bought us kids. We played it so many times that the grooves must have worn thin. The cover itself was as memorable as the song; Dorothée in a striped sweater, posing playfully, while a cartoon drawing of a teasing little brother by the artist Cabu, brought the lyrics to life. We stared at that cover endlessly; the mix of photograph and illustration making it feel like the music itself was alive. That little record didn't just entertain us; it gave us a way to practice our new language, laugh with each other, and feel like we belonged.

Then there were the global hits. In 1982, Musical Youth gave us "Pass the Dutchie," and for the first time we saw kids who looked like us. They had Afros like my brother Emmanuel's and they boasted Caribbean style that felt like home. They were siblings who all looked alike, just like us. Having that type of representation in music and media made us feel seen. Michael Jackson took over in 1983 with "Billie Jean." He wasn't just a star; he was part of a family, and his family dynamic was a major part of his brand. That meant something to my siblings and I. The Jacksons were like a mirror of our own house. We would often imitate the Jackson Five during our play times. We would pick which Jackson we were and reenact their performances. My brother, Emmanuel, was always Michael. It wasn't even a debate. He had that confidence, that spark, and that coolness that rubbed off on all of us. Our playful reenactments made us feel so connected to the Jacksons. We knew what it was like to navigate life with a big family, and I always felt like they were a part of our world. By 1986, Janet Jackson was no longer just Michael Jackson's little sister and backup dancer. She was a star in her own right releasing "What Have You Done for Me

Lately?" full of attitude and style. Then there was Billy Ocean with "When the Going Gets Tough," and Whitney Houston with "How Will I Know." By 1987, Whitney and Michael ruled the charts, but Jody Watley and The Bangles left their mark too. Jody and Janet, especially, were my icons. They were cool, stylish and, confident; the kind of women I looked up to and wanted to model my life after.

Looking back, the funny thing is, we didn't even know the English lyrics to these songs. We sang fake English with pride, making up sounds that matched the lyrics. It didn't matter. Music told us the world was bigger than our little corner of life. Music told us the world was bigger than our little corner of life. It connected us to America; a place that seemed full of possibility and where all the songs and stars we heard about came from. A placed that seemed distant, exciting, and larger than life.

The mid-80s brought more music that shaped us. Tina Turner's "What's Love Got to Do With It" filled the air, strong and unapologetic. Michael's "Thriller" wasn't just a song; it was a whole movement. We copied the moves, laughed at ourselves, and loved every second of it. Stevie Wonder's "I Just Called to Say I Love You" was everywhere too, it was simple, warm and nostalgic. Then came movie soundtracks like, "Ghostbusters" that had us chanting, even though we never saw the film in theaters. In fact, during all our years in France, we only went to the movies once. Entertainment like that simply wasn't part of our routine. That one time we drove into the city to see Snow White felt like the biggest event in the world. Just driving into the city was already exciting. We hardly ever went out at night unless it was for church or maybe a special party for one of our family friends. So riding in the car through Paris after dark felt like stepping into another life. The city glowed; streetlights stretched in neat rows, shop windows lit up as car lights flashed as they passed by.

At the theater, everything was new. I remember being so amazed by the big posters outside, the ticket line and how shiny the theatre was. The smell of fresh buttered popcorn in the air and the smiles of excitement on all of our faces are things I will never forget. We bought a large bag of popcorn to share for the first time. It was so delicious, warm, salty and unlike anything we'd had before. Until then, popcorn had only been something we saw people eating on TV. Now it was ours to savor, and it felt like a small piece of the world we'd only ever imagined before. Then the lights went down, the Disney castle filled the screen, and for that brief moment, we got to sit back and be entertained.

Watching the Disney story unfold was pure magic, but in real life, we were the ones performing; not in a fairy tale, but in church. My parents decided that the six of us would form a singing group. They were convinced it would both glorify God and keep us disciplined. So, after homework and chores, there were mandatory rehearsals. We had harmonies to practice, entrances to coordinate, and songs to memorize before church on Sunday, when we would stand before the congregation in our Sunday best, lined up like a little choir.

That was the real routine. Sundays weren't just another day, Sundays marked the end of the week where the songs we practiced were now ready to be performed. Sundays consisted of getting all six of us ready in coordinated outfits, sitting through long church services that seemed to stretch on forever, and then lingering afterwards as the adults socialized and planned for the next week. My siblings and I hardly watched television, and even when we did, it was limited. The stage we knew best was in front of the church pews, where our voices and matching smiles were expected to shine.

We weren't just part of the service; we were the show. While I couldn't name it then, that was the beginning of a pattern for me. Performing, pleasing, and even earning applause. It was my first taste of what it felt like to win approval by delivering something polished. What started as church performances would grow into a lifelong drive: always working to gain favor, to succeed, and to collect accolades.

GUERDY, AGE 2 ½, MEUDON-LA-FOREST, FRANCE

THE RÉJOUIS KIDS, MEUDON-LA-FOREST, FRANCE

**GUERDY & BROTHER, GRANDMA ALINA,
PARENTS WITH FRIENDS, FRANCE**

Chapter 3
THE RÉJOUIS RULES

That little church singing group my parents formed out of the six of us kids was where it all began. If there was any inspiration, it probably came from *The Sound of Music*. It was a film about a family of seven children, two boys and five girls, just like us. Eventually, there would be seven of us too, but by the time my youngest sister was born, she wouldn't have to live through this routine, because we were already on our way into a whole new world in Miami. The Von Trapp children were guided by their father, Captain Georg von Trapp, a decorated naval officer whose stern discipline reminded me of my own father and his role as a Pastor. Just like in the movie, we too were often dressed in matching outfits and expected to present ourselves as a picture of unity.

The funny part is, we had never given my parents any real reason to think we wanted to sing, except for maybe those moments when we messed around with pop tunes from the '80s, singing them a cappella with more enthusiasm than polished talent. But we were just having fun, not trying to audition for any roles. Around the house, no one was humming in the kitchen or belting out solos in the shower. Music wasn't a calling; it was more of an assignment. In hindsight, that was the first taste of what I call *The Réjouis Rules*: once a decision was made, we followed without question. And once my parents decided we would start singing as a group in church, there was no conversation. We didn't love it or hate it; we didn't even process it. Feelings weren't part of the equation. We simply stood where we were told, sang what we were told to sing, and kept it moving because that's what obedience looked like in our home.

Since I was the youngest, I was always up front and close enough for everyone to see me trying my best to keep up with my older siblings. I copied their mouths, watched their hands and waited for their cues. If my voice couldn't carry, my chubby face did its part, with my round cheeks, smiling confidently. People seemed to like that. If I didn't add much sound, I added presence, and somehow that counted. Looking back now, I realize that was Confidence 101. Being placed front and center taught me how to stand in the spotlight, even when I didn't feel ready. Maybe that's why I can rock a bald head today. Aside from medical reasons and convenience, the comfort I have today doesn't come from trying to prove anything; it comes from not giving a damn what people think about it.

On top of homework, daily chores, and all the after-school extracurriculars; rehearsals were added to the mix. We didn't perform just Sundays either. We performed every Sunday morning and sometimes in the evenings too, and even during midweek services, whenever my father felt the congregation needed a little dose of his children's harmony.

But the only time we really sang with excitement was during Christmas. The streets of Paris were lit with decorations, the shop windows sparkled, and sometimes there was even snow on the ground, making the lights glow brighter. The church was dressed with garlands and nativity scenes, and evening services felt different. We walked through the city under those lights and it felt cozy, almost magical. There were plays, skits, and extra programs for the kids, and that made everything more exciting. My favorite was singing *Petit Papa Noël*. It gave me that warm, "ti kokobe" feeling, (a word I'll explain later in this chapter.)

The real payoff for all that singing wasn't applause or praise, it was French fries. My father would hand us a few francs after service, and we'd bolt down the street to a Turkish vendor whose fries were legendary. He piled them high in a brown paper bag; the grease immediately soaking through until the bag grew translucent. You could smell them before you reached the corner; that irresistible scent of salt and oil filling the air. They were overly salted, but somehow just right; they were golden and crisp on the outside, with a warm, tender center that made each bite perfect.

Whoever was chosen to go buy the French fries never went alone; it was always two of us, a duo. Every Sunday the pairs rotated so everyone had their turn. Even in something as small as a snack run, the rules of fairness applied. The fries were passed out one at a time, like communion, so no one got more than the other. Everything got split evenly. That was *The Réjouis Rules*.

Our entire lives then, revolved around the Haitian philosophy of *Lekòl, Legliz, Lakay;* school, church, home. Those were the three pillars of life in a religious Haitian household. These were *The Réjouis Rules*. If we weren't at school, we were at church. If we weren't at church, we were at home. There was no such thing as free time or idle wandering. The Ten Commandments were not just taught to us at Sunday service; they were enforced at home like an invisible constitution. Between those commandments and *The Réjouis Rules*, there was never much room for bending or breaking.

The effect was double-edged. On one hand, it built a foundation of truth and integrity that I carry to this day. On the other hand, it often made us misfits. At school, while other kids bent rules, we always held back. In the back of our minds was that ever-present voice whispering, *Don't forget who you are. Don't forget what's expected of you.* Being pastor's kids meant every move was watched and every mistake magnified. It was a constant performance. We were on stage even when there was no stage. That too was part of *The Réjouis Rules*.

That shaped me deeply. I became loyal to truth in a way that overpowered my need to fit in. I couldn't fake it; not with friends, not later with women's groups, not in school and not in life. My loyalty to truth often left me on the outside. But it also became a strength and something I would cherish. It made me unwilling to conform and unwilling to bend to the comfort of the crowd. Even today, I stand on the philosophy that "What's right is right, what's wrong is wrong." It meant I walked in my own lane and stayed there, even when the road was lonely. That stubborn truth-telling was both my burden and my compass.

But life wasn't all strictness. There were moments of joy, family, and of adventure. Our little singing group gained popularity in the church circuit, and soon we were invited to sing at other congregations. One of the most unforgettable trips we ever took was a road trip from Paris to Switzerland. All nine of us crammed into a gray Oldsmobile Cutlass Cruiser. It was my parents, Grandma Alina, six children, and our black-and-white cat, Polie. His name meant "polite," though I can't remember who decided that. It was a long station wagon, the kind with a back row that faced the rear window. The smallest kids, like me, were stuck back there. Somehow, we made it work. With our knees pulled in and elbows knocking; everyone squeezed tight, and Polie tucked into whatever corner was left.

The drive felt long but exciting. Out the window I saw fields and small towns. When we got closer to Switzerland, everything looked cleaner and sharper. The water looked clearer, the mountains stood out more, and the air even smelled fresher. I kept my face pressed to the glass the whole way, just watching. When we reached the border, though, we were stopped cold. Switzerland required pet permits, and Polie had none. The officers refused to let the cat in. My father was faced with an impossible choice: turn us all back or find another way. The Swiss Border Patrol gave him special access to drop us off inside Switzerland while they held Polie at the border. He left us there, then drove back with Grandma Alina to return the cat to France.

The truth? Grandma didn't care one bit. In fact, she was relieved. She had never been impressed with French culture, let alone curious about Swiss mountains or lakes. Her joy came from nesting at home and prepping jars of epis seasoning; pounding garlic, herbs, and peppers together until the whole apartment filled with their sharp aroma. In her eyes, Switzerland could keep its views and fresh air, she preferred the comfort of her kitchen. It was a blessing in disguise for her, and she probably thought she got the better end of the deal.

For us kids, though, Switzerland felt like another dimension. The streets looked too clean to be real, like someone scrubbed them every morning. Even the train stations shined. Flowers spilled out of window boxes, mountains stood in the distance, and the lakes were so clear they looked like glass. To me, it felt like a storybook come to life.

But Switzerland wasn't just pretty, it was strict. They fined people for littering, which we had never heard of. Dropping a candy wrapper on the ground could cost you money. That kind of order felt familiar. In Switzerland, the way the streets were kept in line reminded me of *The Réjouis Rules,* clear, fair, and non-negotiable. Years later I learned that Switzerland was one of the first countries to take pollution seriously. Long before people talked about "going green," they were already protecting their air and water. It was part of their culture. Walking those streets felt like stepping into the future.

The next day, my father rejoined us in Switzerland after leaving Polie safely in France with Grandma. Looking back, that moment showed exactly who he was: always willing to go out of his way, balancing love with logistics, to make sure everyone was cared for. In its own way, even that was part of *The Réjouis Rules;* sacrifice, fairness, and doing whatever it took to keep the family moving forward.

Church wasn't just where we sang. It was woven into our daily lives; blended so seamlessly with home and school that it became part of everything we did. The congregation felt like extended family. I remember French women from church coming to our apartment to teach baking classes. My older sisters joined in, and I always tagged along, eager to be the taster. The smell of madeleines baking in the oven is still etched in my memory. That sweet, buttery aroma filled every corner, making the whole apartment feel like a warm blanket. Waiting for the oven timer to buzz was torture. When it finally rang, we'd rush to taste the treats while they were still warm, the outside golden, and the inside soft.

One memory from those baking days always makes me laugh. One of my twin sisters had a habit, not of sucking her thumb, but of sucking the first three fingers of her hand all at once, as if that was her way to self-soothe. One afternoon she was sitting on the sofa, waiting for cookies to finish baking with her fingers in her mouth as usual. My grandmother, who never baked and only stuck to Haitian food, hovered in the kitchen like a guard on duty. She treated those French baking lessons as if her territory was being invaded, standing by with her arms crossed, eyeing the women like warriors who had taken over her domain. Watching my sister on the couch, she finally shook her head and scolded sharply in Creole: "kokobe" or crippled. She told her to stop sucking her fingers, as if it made her look deformed.

That was the first time the word entered our home. At first it was just kokobe, but we were little, so we added "ti" in front of it. Ti kokobe was born and it stuck. Somewhere along the way, the scolding turned into something softer. It became part of our family language. At the sound of it, we knew it meant to come close, cuddle, and get cozy. It was especially a thing during the Christmas holidays, when we'd pile together inside to snuggle warmly.

It was innocent, always. For us, ti kokobe never meant what it actually meant. It was comfort, it was family, it was home. And while it wasn't officially one of *The Réjouis Rules*, the unity it created fit right into the rulebook. Staying unified as a family was a rule above all others, and maybe that's why our parents never corrected us. Letting us keep this word was their way of allowing a bond that could always bring us back together, even years later, through distance, change, and loss.

Those at-home church-lady gatherings had a dual purpose. It was a time to bake and a time to engage in candid conversations. The women flipped through French magazines and gossiped about fashion and royalty, because back in the '80s, royals were celebrities. Princess Diana and Prince Charles were everywhere. The buzz of their upcoming wedding filled pages with stories about what was happening behind the palace walls. It was front-page news all over the world, and the women in our living room followed it like a soap opera.

If we had still been in Haiti, church life might have been far stricter with little room for such casual mixing. But in France, religion and daily life blended more easily. That balance created the kind of normalcy where faith was still central, but there was also space for lightness, curiosity, and even a little glamour. My mother loved all things girly; clothes, jewelry, glamour, and a good fairytale. So it makes sense that one day would stand out above the rest: July 29, 1981, the day Princess Diana married Prince Charles.

That day transformed my mother. I was told that she sat glued to the television, transfixed. For her, Diana wasn't just a royal on the screen, she was proof that a woman could rise, be admired and elevated with no limits. My mother had always been ambitious, but Diana's wedding ignited something in her. From that moment, she carried herself differently, dressed differently, and even dreamed differently. She adopted what I now call the "no finishing line" mentality; a drive that trickled down to us kids, for better and worse. Years later, after giving birth to my youngest sister in 1987, she even had my father buy her a replica of Diana's sapphire engagement ring as a push present. It was her way of owning a piece of that fairytale.

My mother was a force. She was fashion-forward, relentless and impossible to ignore. She hoarded clothes, hats, jewelry, and decorations. More was always better. Diana became her muse, and watching that wedding gave my mother a new hunger. She wanted to be admired too. She wanted to host, to showcase, to prove she had built something worthy of attention, and she did. In just three years, we moved from a cramped three-bedroom apartment to a six bedroom, two-story house near Versailles.

Her pride showed in aesthetics. It was loud and bold. She dressed us with care and drilled her motto into us: "Dress how you want to be addressed." It wasn't just a saying, it was another *Réjouis Rule*. We overdressed for everything, church, school, errands and visitors. It wasn't vanity. It was armor. As the pastor's children, we couldn't afford flaws. Presentation was everything, and she documented it all. We had albums upon albums stacked high, and crammed with family portraits showcasing coordinated outfits. Looking back, those photos were her way of preserving joy, of proving our come up, and of reminding us she was a good mother. Page after page, it looked like a storybook.

When we moved into the new house, it wasn't just moving on up, it was keeping up with the 'Dubois' (the French equivalent of the Joneses). My mother's personality filled inside as much as it spilled to the outside. The décor leaned ornate, almost stuck in the 18th century, like something out of the Sisi of Austria days. But it wasn't authentic or antique, it was the replica version; the cheaper kind that mimicked the style without the price tag. In a way, it was a little wannabe, but in her eyes, it was elegant, and she treated it with the same pride as if it had come straight from a palace. Haitians have a way of preserving furniture, (maybe it's an island thing,) by covering it in plastic so no one dares stain it. The irony, of course, was that the beauty was muted under the plastic, but the instinct to protect it outweighed the desire to enjoy it freely.

The inside was impressive, but the outside, at first, was just a plain canvas. The yard had nothing on it but grass. No flowers, no stones, no ornaments. What it did have was potential and a natural mound that gave it dimension, almost like it was waiting to be shaped. And my mother, who had seen the grandeur of the Versailles gardens, was about to play fairy godmother. If Versailles could have layered beauty, then so could we.

That's where the partnership of my parents came into play. My mother was the ambitious one, always pushing for more, and always seeing what could be. And my father, the one who would do anything for her, took that vision and built it piece by piece, paycheck by paycheck. Together they turned that blank yard into something extraordinary.

He stacked stones into steps that climbed the mound, leading to a small opening gate at the very top, where we could step through and reach the other side of the neighborhood. In other words, a shortcut. We would use it to save time when walking to school. My mother directed the look and feel, and my father delivered it with his hands. It was her very own Versailles, created for her by him. Soon, bright flowers filled the space. Reds, yellows, pinks, and purples layered against green shrubs climbing the stones. She loved tulips and roses. Vegetation also spilled across the yard in waves, where we grew strawberries and herbs. And then came the decorative ducks. Dozens of white plastic ducks scattered across the hill like lawn royalty, announcing to anyone passing by that this was no ordinary garden.

Cars slowed to stare. Strangers driving through the neighborhood for their first time pulled over just to admire. For a working-class family in a brand new neighborhood, it was completely abnormal to have a yard like ours. Honest to God, it could have rivaled any botanical garden. And that, too, reflected The *Réjouis Rules:* if you were going to do something, you did it right, and you sure as hell did it all the way.

And context mattered. At that time, this newly constructed neighborhood didn't have any Black families moving in. Diversity existed, but it was scarce. There were mostly traditional French households, with the exception of one Algerians family where the husband had 3 wives. For us, stepping into that environment meant we were surrounded by neighbors who didn't look like us and who lived lives more grounded in French tradition. This move, this house, this garden; it was our arrival into what was considered the middle class. And my parents wanted everyone who passed our yard to know: the Réjouis family was here too. Looking back now, I think that boldness and being loud, proud, and unapologetic about who we were shaped me more than I realized. It's part of why I can sit in a room full of people of different races, whether they look like me or not, and feel completely at ease. That confidence didn't come from blending in. It came from standing out.

Taking it a step further, our parents put up an obstacle-course gym playset in the backyard, which became the stage for our own "Olympics." When the Olympic Games aired on television, we rushed outside to reenact them, especially the gymnastics and races led by Emmanuel, our oldest brother. At more than six feet tall, he always won. To us, it wasn't even a competition, of course Emmanuel would take the crown. He was always our champion. Today, I see so much of him in my son Liam, who at twelve has already shot up to six feet himself, carrying that same quiet dominance.

The rules in our house weren't cut and clear, but they were understood. At the center of them was this: always strive to be the best version of yourself. That silent expectation shaped everything. The comparisons between us kids were quieter, almost unspoken, but we all felt them. There were always subtle reminders of who had the better grades, who sang the best, or who carried themselves more properly. It was never loud, but it was always there like an unspoken code, another layer of *The Réjouis Rules*.

Even as a pastor's wife, my mother adored television shows like *Dallas* and *Dynasty*. They were her escape. Maybe it tied back to her childhood, having grown up in Catholic boarding schools where she was expected to be a goody-two-shoes, always following the rules. She never had the freedom to explore "the other side" of life for herself. Watching those shows as an adult gave her a glimpse into that world; a world of glamour, betrayal, ambition, and excess.

It was an oxymoron, really. By day, she was the wife of a strict religious man, surrounded by sermons about humility, modesty, and self-denial. By night, she was glued to the television, taking in storylines filled with lust, greed, wealth, and status. Everything about *Dallas* and *Dynasty* stood in direct contradiction to the message of the pulpit. And yet, my mother never missed an episode. She wasn't living through the characters, and she wasn't trying to be them. It was more about curiosity and about seeing what the other side looked like. And maybe, over time, the takeaway became this: that ambition, excess, and drama weren't as far-fetched as they seemed. That they could exist, even in her own life, in her own way. Princess Diana fed into the same current. Between Diana's real-life fairytale and the TV queens of prime time, my mother absorbed a new message: there was nothing wrong with wanting more. Luxury, ambition and beauty; they weren't sins. They were aspirations.

That's where the difference between my parents showed most clearly. My father was the one who believed in truly "turning the other cheek," following the Bible almost word for word, and keeping life simple. My mother would turn the cheek too, but she might slap back, just like Alexis on *Dynasty*. For her, fairness sometimes mattered more than being "the bigger person." She wouldn't let herself be bullied, and she didn't think anyone else should either. That attitude, I later realized, wasn't such a bad thing. It planted a seed in me that I would only fully appreciate years later, after betrayal found its way into my own life, (a story I'll get to much later), during a time when I learned who my true friends were.

When I look back now, I think that same striving; that ambition to be the best version of ourselves, is what caused tension in the church world too. On the surface, people should want to aim high. But when they saw it happening in front of them, and it wasn't happening for them, it became a threat. Envy brewed, and I believe that was part of why my family had to move from one church to another. We looked like "the family who made it," and not everyone liked that. And just like in the shows my mother watched, Dallas and Dynasty, pettiness thrived. Egos battled for the spotlight, jealousy hid behind forced smiles, and hypocrisy often preached louder than the gospel. All while dressed in the language of righteousness but rooted in competition. Behind the scenes, the church could be as cutthroat as prime-time television.

Those experiences taught me a truth I carry with me: church people are still people. Even those who preach holiness can act like the very heathens they warn against. By the time I left for college, I was ready to find God on my own terms, and I did. What I carried forward was this unspoken lesson of The Réjouis Rules: when others fall short, don't let it shake who you are.

THE RÉJOUIS FAMILY, PARIS, FRANCE 1980

THE RÉJOUIS SISTERS SINGING IN A CHURCH

Chapter 4

M.I.A. IN MIAMI

France ignited something in my parents. My parents' dreams were larger than life, and throughout their lives, they would end up trying to realize each of them, whether realistic or not. My father, I think, particularly exhausted himself trying to fulfill both her happiness while trying to fulfill his own spiritual purpose.

As for me, I finally tasted what it felt like to be rooted. France wasn't just where we lived, it was where we belonged. Paris had become our stage, our training ground, our kingdom. I felt like a girl with purpose. My confidence was high, and I had inherited a lot of my mom's ways. My mother never let wrongs go unchecked. If someone received better treatment than she did at a department store, she spoke up. If someone tried to skip ahead in line, she would clear her throat, raise her chin, and clock it. She didn't yell. She didn't need to. Her confidence was a lighthouse in any room, and her sense of justice was unwavering. Her French was impeccable; she was an avid reader, and through that came these big words that maybe the French didn't expect to hear out of her mouth. But there she was, babbling away and taking no prisoners. That righteous flame she passed down to me became my superpower. Maybe even my burden. Because once you know your value, you can't unknow it.

To this day, my mom recounts the stories of me being a natural leader in primary school. I don't know if I was born with it as the doctor in Port-au-Prince had told my mom; that I would become someone special in the world. Or if it was the product of my mom's ways rubbing off on me. Maybe a little of both. But I was the leader of the class from the very beginning of attending primary school. I remember being looked up to by a lot of the kids and it wasn't because of what I had, since we were middle-class equals, but because of the confidence I carried. The teacher herself would sometimes use me to set the tone in the classroom and get the kids' attention. Sometimes she would place me on top of her desk and say, "Listen to Elischéba." I spoke with the same boldness I had witnessed in my mother, and I would demand that everyone be quiet.

It even went a step further. I was somewhat of a tomboy when it was convenient; coquette at times, tomboy at others; and as I advanced from grade to grade, people came to me if they were being bullied. I would, with no shame, go up to the girl or boy, even challenge them, but not in a physical way. I would confront them with logic and reasoning so they would know that justice would come at all costs. My boldness alone made it stop. Yes, I was one of the tallest kids, but very skinny. So it wasn't about my size, but more so about the authoritative way I carried myself. I was channeling survivors and people unafraid to step into uncharted territories. I was the product of my parents and of my ancestors. Or perhaps that fire subconsciously sparked on that quiet day I sat on a cold tile floor next to my grandma Alina, lost, in that apartment lobby. Somewhere deep inside, I made a vow: never again. Never again would I feel unseen. France made that vow feel possible. There, I was somebody; loud, loved, and listened to.

In our household, family meetings weren't casual conversations over dinner, they were structured, official, and filled with weight. My father, a man of strong presence and purpose, would gather us all in the living room and stand as if about to give a sermon in church. My mother would sit beside him, her eyes moving between us kids with a kind of quiet strength. These meetings were where plans were made for the future; where things got real. School performances, church events, chores, discipline, and upcoming changes in the family were just some of the topics. And when we slipped up, discipline came. My mother tattled on our every wrong move, warning us with her signature line, "Wait till Papa comes home." Usually there was more than one culprit, because in our household if one of us did something, another sibling was usually involved. My father would use his belt, sometimes making me extend my hands while he struck them. As I got older, I built a tolerance. I became what Haitians call frekan or fresh; a smart mouth. I would stare him straight in the eyes, pretending it didn't hurt, silently telling him he wouldn't win.

One night during one of those family meetings, my father made an announcement that cracked the very foundation of our world. "We're moving to America." Just like that. No buildup. No warning. He explained it was for religious reasons. My father's deep religious and cultural connection with Haiti was always noticeable, nostalgic even. Back in Haiti, he had been on the verge of emerging as a major figure in the church. The political environment and unrest had stripped that chance from him, and it felt as though he was always trying to avenge that loss. He told us he had reconnected with a relative he grew up with in Haiti who was now in Miami with his own congregation. This relative bragged about how amazing America was; full of promised opportunities, a better future, and new chapters to be unfolded.

At that moment everything he said seemed like a blur. His mouth was moving and words were coming out but I only heard one word: "America". That word hit differently. America wasn't just a place; it was *the* place. The land of dreams, neon lights and legends. It was where Michael Jackson reigned. Where Whitney Houston triumphed. Where Disney wasn't just a movie studio, but an entire magical kingdom called Disney World. To me, that was enough to feel like we were chosen. We bragged to our classmates that we were moving to Miami. To Disney World! We spoke as if we'd already been there and met Mickey Mouse himself. It didn't matter that there were no concrete details yet. Just the promise was enough.

But my mother opposed the plan. She had built a home in France, with friends, routine, and a life that finally felt like stability. By this point, we had a well-oiled machine of a household. Our lives and her friendships that she treasured. Why start over again? Still, she eventually gave in. She knew that if she didn't, my father would resent her. She was confident that if she had built a life once, she could do it again. But she would never miss a chance to compare what we left behind in France to what we were heading into in Miami.

Shortly after this big news, we celebrated my parents' wedding anniversary with a small party. It was just a few close family friends and our large family, which already made nine of us. It was May 9, 1986, and I was eight years old. It felt less like an anniversary party and more like a final hooray; a family gathering where everyone was happy at the same time, before everything began to change. I wore a light pink ruffled dress and my hair was freshly twisted with "boul gogo" bobbles. Of course we took the ceremonial family photos for my mother's albums. When I look at that album now, I see myself sitting with my legs crossed , smiling wide, and with so much composure for my age.

Till this day, I don't know why my mom allowed me to wear lipstick at that party. I was too young, people would say. Was it because my mother knew, from her own childhood of being sent away, that I too would soon have to grow up quickly for survival, just as she once had to? Was it her way of letting me enjoy one last taste of innocence before life shifted? I'll never know. My mother never talked about her own experience of being sent away to Catholic school. She liked the sense of notoriety that being taught by the nuns at Catholic school in Haiti carried, but she never revealed what it had done to her as a little girl. Did she feel abandoned too? Did it make her feel like she wasn't worthy of staying at home with her siblings? For a young mind, not knowing or understanding the reasons for your parents' choices could feel torturous.

The day came in the summer of 1987. Saying goodbye was grief. My mother stood with the newest and seventh member of the Réjouis clan, my baby sister, in her arms. I had mixed feelings. On one hand, I was relieved not to be the baby anymore. On the other, being sent away right after she was born not only made me feel displaced; it made me feel like I was being replaced. None of that mattered in the moment, though. What weighed on me was leaving my grandmother; my anchor. Her hands were small, cold, and rough, worn from years of labor. Her blue cataract-clouded eyes followed me as I walked away. She never said "I love you", but I felt it in every gesture, especially when she pressed food into my hands for the plane ride. That was her love language. She watched silently as I left, and I felt the weight of it in my chest. My mother, by contrast, was emotional and dramatic, her pain spilling out like a soap opera scene. Sometimes I'd look at the two of them together, polar opposites from the same lineage, and wonder how I fit between them. I definitely took after my mother, though sometimes I wished I was more balanced.

On the plane, it was just me, my father, and my brother Joel. At first, I must admit the journey was exciting. I had only flown once before, from Haiti to Paris when we fled Duvalier's Haiti, but I was too young to remember it. I had never been one to want many toys; I was an old soul, more interested in setting up Barbie's house than playing with Barbie herself. Maybe that was the first hint of my desire to control environments and the seed of my future career. But for this trip, I brought a teddy bear to be my travel buddy. My plush pal represented a piece of home. I pressed it against the window as the clouds drifted by us. But when we landed, there were no bright lights, no Disney, no music. It was afternoon in Miami, and all I felt was the heavy heat, the flat horizon, palm trees and the strangeness of the new city.

We arrived at our relative's house in Allapattah, Miami. This was the same relative who had marveled at the American Dream. This was the place where the three of us; my father, my brother Joel, and I, would stay. At first, we didn't grasp what was really happening. The house felt temporary, like a stopover, and we told ourselves this was just part of the journey. But when my father finally stood at the door with his luggage in hand a few days later, the truth sank in. And then it all became reality: he was leaving us.

He kissed us goodbye and repeated the words he had already drilled into us, *"Don't embarrass the family."* And we listened, because our family name was the only thing we had. In Haitian culture, reputation, honor, and family pride are the most valuable things you can carry, and we knew that even as children. That was the essence of the *Réjouis Rules*. It explained why our parents dressed us the way they did, why they pushed us so hard. We were tokens in a sense; living proof of their success, the children they could present to the world as evidence that they had made it. But now, dropped into uncharted territory, our pride collided with our new reality. In this house, we didn't feel like proof of anything.

To us, they were strangers; fresh faces we had never met before, yet suddenly we were required to live under their roof. It was our relative, his wife, their daughter, and their son. From the start, the air felt different. Not hostile, but not welcoming either. The wife carried herself with a coldness that reminded me in some ways of my grandmother Alina, except with Alina I knew how to translate her silences as love. With this woman, I couldn't read her. Her stillness felt like a standoff, and I never wanted to do anything that might upset her. She gave me chores to do around the house, not like Cinderella, but just enough to keep me busy. It helped the days move along, each one feeling like a slow countdown until my father would come back for us.

Their daughter, sadly, had cerebral palsy. She was a sweet seven year old girl, yet still in diapers because of her condition. She was completely nonverbal, her face fixed in a frozen expression that never shifted no matter the circumstance. Sometimes it looked like a smile, but it wasn't. She would often drool, twitch, and let out a steady moan that never stopped. It was a drawn-out sound that lingered in the air like white noise. Her hands rubbed together repetitively, almost in a loop, as if her body couldn't break free from the motions. She paced slowly around the house, following us wherever we went, her eyes locked on us as though she was trying to communicate but couldn't. At times she would bump into us, drooling on our arms, or lean too far forward and collapse onto us, and we would lift her back up, steadying her small frame so she didn't fall again. It was constant. She was always there, always moving, always making that sound.

No one ever explained what her condition was. No one told us what we were seeing, or what it meant, or how we could support her. We were just children, and being left without understanding made it confusing and overwhelming. Her sounds filled the house, repetitive and inescapable, a constant reminder of how little I understood of the world around me.

Their son added to that weight. In contrast, he was spoiled, smug, and loud in his own confidence. He was like that greedy boy from *Charlie and the Chocolate Factory,* always needing attention, always performing. When he came home from school, he'd swing the door open with a swagger, and toss his book bag down like a trophy, as if the simple act of attending school gave him superiority over us. There was a smug rhythm in his step, a kind of parade announcing, "I belong here, and you don't."

He got a kick out of the fact that we didn't speak English. Our silence made him feel bigger. He would sit at the table and overperform in everything; reading his homework assignments aloud, scribbling furiously, and sighing loudly as if to remind us that he had access to something we didn't. I had never in my life envied homework, but when something is taken away from you, you crave it more than ever. Watching him flaunt what he had only reminded me of what we didn't. It made me long for the routine of school, even the assignments and books. Sometimes, when we watched cartoons together, his sister would wander in front of the television, her body moving unpredictably. Instead of being patient with her, he'd shoo her away dismissively. It wasn't violent, but it was dismissive. I didn't like him. He never translated for us when we asked what was happening on TV; he'd wave us off, saying to just watch, as if language didn't matter. His indifference stung because we already felt so left out.

Meals drove the point home even more. He always got second helpings, while my brother and I stayed quiet with what we were served. We never asked for more; our parents had drilled into us the importance of manners, so we behaved small. The less noticeable we were, the better. Meanwhile, their son was loud and free, taking up space, while we folded ourselves into the background. He was everything we couldn't be; visible, vocal, and entitled; and he loved it.

The days themselves fell into the same routine, over and over. Each day looked like the one before with each moment dragging, slow and repetitive. There was no school to break up the monotony, just time that seemed to stretch endlessly. In the middle of all that monotony were the plantain chips. Not just a snack, but the only snack. Every single day. The same yellow package, the same dry crunch, the same salty taste. Over and over. Small yellow bags filled with dry, salty slices that became our constant in-between meals. It felt endless, like we were on some kind of punishment. For three long months, whenever hunger crept in, the answer was the same: plantain chips. At first, they seemed like a treat, but soon they tasted like punishment. If disaster prep had been a thing back then, we would've been set, we had plantain chips for days, for weeks, for months. Hell, for a lifetime. To this day, I can't even stand the sight of them in a grocery store aisle. The only plantain chips I'll eat are the freshly fried ones from Cuban restaurants like La Carreta.

The plantain chips were stored in the garage, a place that always felt intimidating. Because my father's relative was a pastor, it was filled with boxes of donated food for the church. There were always cans stacked tall in aisles that were dark and dusty. I hated stepping in there by myself, always bracing for a rat to dart out of the shadows. Sometimes I stood in the doorway while my brother dashed inside to grab a bag, like we were planning a heist.

The backyard should have been our refuge, but it wasn't. What was once a pool had turned into a murky pond, filled with green water and overrun by frogs. At night, their croaking grew so loud it felt like it was echoing inside my head. From that sound, I built a lifelong phobia of frogs, lizards, and snakes; honestly anything that slithered or jumped. Every shuffle in the bushes made me freeze.

The front yard, however, was a different world altogether. The street was alive with kids playing; their laughter and shouts spilling into the house. The ice cream truck rolled by daily, its cheerful jingle would float through the humid air. Cars rumbled past with that Miami bass sound booming so hard it shook the pavement; each one more flamboyant than the last, with bright colors, flashy rims, and speakers commanding attention. The neighborhood was predominantly African-American and full of energy and life. But I only watched it all from behind the glass. If we already felt like outsiders inside the house, imagine stepping out there. It was the most frightening thought: longing to belong, yet knowing we wouldn't. The fear of being bullied for being different, for not knowing the language, for being unable to blend in, kept us inside. And so we stayed, suffocated by the walls, the silence, and the heat.

The one breath of relief came from my uncle, my mother's younger brother, who lived nearby in Little Haiti. Even though he wasn't very reliable, as he would often promise to visit and then never show. Whenever he did appear, the entire atmosphere shifted and suddenly, we could breathe again. Looking back, I now realize he had his own struggles. I couldn't pinpoint it as a child, but you could sense he had "lived" what people today might call being "outside." Still, none of that mattered to us. He was kind, like his mother, my grandmother Alina. He didn't speak much, just barked short commands like, "let's go," "get in the car," "take this," "bring that" and that was enough. He didn't have children of his own, and it showed. He wasn't fatherly like my dad; instead, he treated us like buddies, and we loved it. To us, it felt just right. He even looked like my mom, despite one of his eyes being slightly crossed and glasses perched on his face. To me, that made him even more endearing. He was cool. And for those few hours with him, when he whisked us away from that house to see a sliver of Miami, we felt cool too.

He would scoop us up and take us to McDonald's. I still remember biting into my first cheeseburger like it was yesterday. The taste of the salty fries and even the orange soda brought us the joy of feeling normal. Sometimes he'd switch it up with Popeyes

Chicken, and that's when I fell in love with spicy food. Afterward, we'd head to his small apartment in Little Haiti, right on 54th Street and 2nd Avenue. That corner was like the Mecca for Haitians, you could feel the pride of being surrounded by our people. For my uncle, it must have felt good to be in the center of it, and for us, it was a comfort. I'm grateful for that time because it gave my brother and I the chance to practice our Creole. Even now, we speak it better than our other siblings, all because of those three months.

The apartment itself was bare and small, probably just a short-term rental, and it had no air conditioning. But to us, it was paradise. Any new environment outside that house, or church on Sundays, was good enough. He shared it with his girlfriend at the time, who looked EXACTLY like Esther Rolle, the actress who played the mother in *Good Times*. She was intimidating, mysterious, and clearly the boss in that relationship. She was twice his size and looked years older than him, but he adored her. You could see it written all over his face. He'd flip on the TV, and we'd watch wrestling together. Hulk Hogan was his obsession, and because he loved it, we loved it too. We sat cross-legged on the floor, screaming at the screen, caught up in the drama and the theatrics. One time he even took us to the beach. For those few hours, we were happy, curious, and unafraid. We were just kids again, laughing with our uncle, drowning in fast food and joy.

But then, like clockwork, just like Cinderella at midnight, he'd drive us back. Out of the three months, he only took us out maybe four times. It was quality over quantity, and we were grateful for every second. Still, the moment the door shut behind us, we were back to confinement, and the cycle began again. As a child, I thought maybe we were being punished, that maybe I wasn't worthy. That interpretation lodged deep inside me.

With the help of therapy today, I've learned to recognize this period of my life for what it was: a core trauma. The abrupt separation from my siblings. The grief of leaving my family. The confusion of living with strangers. The steady drooling, twitching and moans of her condition, which no one explained to us. Their son's bullying; flaunting what we couldn't have. The reptiles that croaked me into phobias. The endless monotony of plantain chips. The ice cream truck jingles and the neighborhood kids, so close yet untouchable. Each one left its mark.

And yet, even as I speak of trauma, I have to hold both truths. The relatives we stayed with weren't warm, but they gave us the basics: food, shelter, and safety. They weren't our parents, but they kept us safe when things could have been much worse. Many children endure far worse; abuse, neglect and even violence. I did not and for that, I am grateful. My parents weren't abandoning me out of malice; they were sacrificing, the same way survival had always demanded in Haiti. It was the rhythm of survival passed down: hard choices, painful separations, and risks taken for the possibility of a better tomorrow.

As a little girl, I couldn't see that. In fact, those traumas planted something in me that would shape the rest of my life: the belief that if I made myself valuable, I wouldn't be dispensable. If I made myself valuable, I would never be forgotten, and I would never be left behind again. That survival tactic would follow me for years. And so I became the fixer, the one who noticed everything, solved everything and carried it all. I was the boss. The one who controlled everything when I realized that no one was going to save me, I decided I would learn to save myself.

Journaling and writing reflective letters was very therapeutic for me. It allowed me to express things that I didn't have the language to express as a little girl. That's what healing does, it empowers you to release the things that we tend to carry that no longer serve the person we've become along the way. Letting go, coming to terms with and even accepting the things that we cannot change is a personal freedom that liberates the heart and mind.

GUERDY, DAY OF WEDDING ANNIVERSARY PARTY AT HOME, MAY 9, 1986

THE RÉJOUIS FAMILY AT HOME, DAY OF WEDDING ANNIVERSARY PARTY AT HOME, MAY 9, 1986

GUERDY AND HER BROTHER EMMANUEL IN MIAMI

Chapter 5
LEARNING TO BELONG

Those three months alone with my brother in Miami didn't just dent my spirit, they cracked it wide open. When the rest of my family finally arrived, I didn't feel joy, I felt shock. My sisters ran to me with their arms open and voices high with excitement. "How was it?" they asked. I don't remember what I said. Maybe I lied and said "okay." Maybe I said nothing at all. But I know that what I wanted to say was: Why did you leave us? Why me? Why him? However, at the time I decided those questions had no place in the reunion hugs and the happy noise. So, I swallowed them.

My father found a small house with three bedrooms and a Florida room, which we converted into a room for my brothers. A Florida room, as I later learned, is a space attached to the house, often at the back, designed to let in as much sunlight as possible. It was definitely an American thing as we had nothing like that in France. Though it was a huge adjustment considering we had come from a two-story, six-bedroom house with a yard that felt like a park, this new house suited us. Our youngest sister, still in a crib, stayed with my parents in their room, my brothers were together in the Florida room, the twins in one room while I was paired in the last room with my oldest sister. I think the plan was that as the older children advanced in school and eventually left for college, the rest of us would play musical chairs with the rooms, shifting beds and arrangements as needed.

Moving from a large house to a small one threw us into what I call "predetermined hoarding mode." Nothing was to scale. There wasn't enough room in this new house for all the fragile, oversized furniture my parents insisted on bringing, and certainly not for my mother's extensive wardrobe. But somehow, they managed to cram everything that they brought, including their massive bed set with a huge armoire. That arrangement left only slivers of walking space around the perimeter of the master bedroom.

The house was in North Miami, directly across from Holy Family Catholic Church. The neighborhood was diverse; two Haitian families, a couple of Cuban families, and the rest white Americans. There were plenty of children to play with, and because there were so many of us, we quickly dominated the street by numbers. The language barrier wasn't as frightening anymore, because at least we had each other.

Before my brother and I left France for Miami, my oldest sibling, Emmanuel, had just returned from an exchange program in England where he had been living with an English family. One of the things he brought home with him was a set of English-learning audio cassette tapes. My ever resourceful mother had the idea to prep us for Miami by making us listen to and repeat after the teacher on the audio cassette. Back then, cassette tapes were the newest thing, so we were excited to actually have and be using them. A woman's voice would recite a word or sentence, and we'd repeat it over and over again.

The only phrases I actually remember learning were: "How do you do?" and "I'm very well, thank you." I thought I had cracked the code and that this was my golden ticket into the English language. I was convinced that once we landed, I would be cool and get to say that to someone. But no one ever asked me that. From the moment we arrived, the only greeting I received from anyone was simply "hi". What was "hi"? This was not mentioned in the cassette tapes that we had listened to so attentively. I didn't understand it. I was waiting to hear the exact phrase that I had learned, but it never came. My frustration and confusion were overwhelming.

During those three months in Allapattah, my brother and I picked up some English from watching TV every day, but I was at a D–level at best. Still, I hoped and figured I'd learn properly in school, and that thought gave me excitement.

Finally, we would get back to a normal routine like we had in France. Finally, we would get to be kids again. Finally, we would be in a familiar rhythm with our siblings and parents. For me, most importantly, it meant going back into my grandmother's arms to eat her food and to have her take care of me the way she used to. That was all that mattered. But then reality hit: it was time for school.

After what felt like an eternity of waiting, I was finally enrolled. I was hopeful that this would be my reset, my reentry into normal life. Though I was supposed to be in fourth grade, they placed me in third. I didn't understand why. I was nine, and in France I had been ahead of my class. But now I was being treated as though I were behind. No one explained why. Maybe it was standard procedure for foreign students, to see if they matched the American system.

On the enrollment paperwork, my parents put my middle name, Elischéba Réjouis. We had never used my first name, Guerdy. In

France, Elischéba was easy to pronounce and sounded beautiful. I was proud of it. It came from the Bible. My mother added the letter "c" to make it unique, but the traditional spellings were Elisheba or Elisheva. The Greek translation is Elizabeth, which is also where my nickname "Babette" came from. The name itself is of Hebrew origin and means "God is my oath" or "God's promise."

My name, which had flowed so easily from Creole and French lips, became a battlefield for American tongues. In Miami, people fumbled it badly, turning it into a performance. They mispronounced it, teased it, and twisted it, until I began to dread introductions. On the first day, the teacher read it aloud with all the grace of a car crash. She stumbled, paused, tried again, and laughed nervously. The class erupted in laughter, and just like that, I was the punchline. At recess, it got worse. A boy who was a self-proclaimed class clown, started a chant: "Elischebam bam bam!" He sang it every time he saw me and it quickly caught on with my classmates. Laughter followed me like a shadow.

I didn't speak enough English to fight back. The only phrase I could recall from those cassette tapes was, "How do you do? I'm very well, thank you." That was it. And just like that, the same feelings from Allapattah, three months of isolation, awkwardness, and embarrassment took over again. I became the girl who didn't belong. My name was wrong. My food smelled strange. My voice, too unsure. My clothes screamed "other." And my hair, with thick twists weighed down by bright butterfly and star barrettes that clicked with every step, made me stand out even more. Within just a few days, I was pulled from the classroom and placed in ESOL; English for Speakers of Other Languages. It seemed like a holding pen for kids like me, who were caught in the middle of cultural assimilation and suspended between old and new life. We spent half the day in that classroom, returning to our regular classes for art, music, and physical education. The ESOL room was filled with faces from Cuba, Colombia, Venezuela, Haiti, and beyond.

While most of the kids bonded quickly with others from their own countries, I felt different. Yes, I was Haitian, but my mannerisms were unmistakably French. I lived there until I was nine. My French accent was thick when I tried to speak English and even carried into my Creole when I spoke with fellow Haitians. In French, the rhythm of speech is slower, almost like a song, with pauses between words. And when a French person speaks English, they often fill those pauses with a little "uh." So instead of flowing straight through a sentence, you'll hear something like, "I am—uh—going to the store—uh—to buy something." It isn't hesitation; it's just part of the rhythm.

Growing up in France, I never noticed this, but when I arrived in Miami, that "uh" sound and cadence made me stand out immediately. When I tried to befriend Haitian kids, they could tell something was off. To me, Haitians were my people, and I assumed the Haitian community in Miami would embrace me. What I didn't know was that being Haitian in Miami during the eighties carried layers of tension and stigma from the outside world, and even from within the Haitian community itself.

At that time, Miami was flooded with new Haitian arrivals. While my family had left Haiti for France in 1980, others from that same wave migrated directly to Miami and New York. We were all part of the same storm, only scattered in different directions: some to Miami, some to New York, and us to France. Fleeing Duvalier's dictatorship, many came by boat risking everything for survival. By 1987, there were more than 70,000 Haitians in South Florida.

But Haitians weren't given the same welcome Cubans received. Rarely granted asylum, many were locked up in detention centers or deported back. The ones who stayed faced open hostility. Haitians were painted as poor, uneducated, and diseased. In the seventies, rumors tied Haitians to tuberculosis, and at one point, the CDC listed Haitians as a risk group for HIV and AIDS. Even when that was later removed, the damage was already done. To be Haitian in Miami at that time was to carry stigma everywhere you went.

Within the Black community as a whole, Haitians were seen as outsiders. They spoke Creole, not English like Jamaican or Bahamian migrants. African American kids often bullied Haitian students, mocking and beating them, making them feel they didn't belong anywhere. Many Haitian kids tried to hide who they were by refusing to speak Creole, changing their names and adopting African American styles just to avoid exposure. For some, the shame was unbearable. The story of Phede Eugene, a teenager who killed himself in 1984 after being outed as Haitian in front of his girlfriend, haunted the community. It showed how deeply the rejection cut.

Even within the Haitian community itself, divisions remained. In Haiti, class and color had always created lines, and those lines carried over to Miami. Some Haitians considered themselves bourgeois, (wealthier, lighter skinned, or French-speaking) and kept their distance from the less privileged. Speaking French was a quick way to signal class. As a little girl fresh from France, I didn't know any of this, but the moment I opened my mouth, my French accent placed me in that bourgeois box. It didn't matter that my family was dark-skinned or that we were starting over like everyone else. We were judged before we even had the chance to explain.

That was one of the most painful lessons of those early years. It left me floating, unsure where I fit, carrying the sting of rejection before I even knew the rules of this new environment. And while the outside world carried its judgments, I searched for small anchors of belonging. That's when I met my first true friend, Jennifer Melvin.

Jennifer was different. When I say "true friend," I mean someone who wasn't just a friend out of convenience, like many of my ESOL Haitian friends who I bonded with because of our shared struggles. They were my friends too, and I loved them for the comfort of commonality, but Jennifer was something else. We had nothing in common, yet we had a genuine connection. She was American, chubby, and full of sunshine. She wore every shade of Keds sneakers you could think of and matched them with ribbons tied neatly around her ponytail. Her voice was soft and her heart wide open. She never laughed at me, never asked why my food looked weird and never flinched at my name.

She invited me into her home, which felt like a suburban dream compared to the cramped chaos of mine. We sat on her carpet, eating peanut butter sandwiches, watching sitcoms, and giggling at things I barely understood at first. She never knew it, but she was teaching me how to assimilate, not by erasing who I was, but by sharing what she knew. Her world seemed neat and simple. Mine was layered and loud. But somehow, we met in the middle.

Maybe we had more in common than I first realized. She didn't have many friends either. Being chubby set her apart from the so-called "cool kids," just like my accent and background set me apart. Maybe that's how we saw each other, two outsiders looking in on a world passing us by. I like to think of our meeting as divine intervention. In her own way, she helped me integrate into a more "normal" society while still letting me hold onto the twist of my international background. Looking back now, it feels like the early seed of what would become my "traditional with a twist" GUERDYFY brand.

At that point, blending in meant everything to me, because standing out was too painful. Every day I studied the world around me. I watched how people moved, what they wore, how they spoke. I mimicked. I adapted. I blended. Because standing out meant being questioned, and being questioned meant you didn't belong. For the second time in my short life, I had to pivot, adjust, and become a chameleon; again!

By the end of junior high, I had started to find my place. I was semi-fluent in English and more at ease with my surroundings. I could navigate between Haitian, African American, Latino, and white kids without too much trouble. Being raised in France and having lived through multiple migrations had trained me to be adaptable. Adaptability became my survival skill. During this same time however, Haitian hostility in schools was real. By junior high, "Haitian Fridays" had become a weekly event where kids would gang up on Haitian students just for being Haitian. Fights broke out, and Haitian kids were targeted simply for existing. It was terrifying. I was never directly attacked, maybe by luck, maybe by timing, but my parents would still come early to pick us up from school, just in case.

Because of the bullying, some Haitian youth created Zoe Pound as a way to fight back. They called themselves, "Zoe" meaning "bone" or "hard to the bone." "Pound", was an acronym for "Power Of Unified Negroes (in) Divinity" to show they were hard and unbreakable. This movement started in Miami's Little Haiti neighborhood and developed almost as a gang, but over time it grew into something bigger. "Zoe" became a word of pride in the Haitian community, a way of saying we are family, we are strong, and we will never be ashamed of who we are. They helped shift the culture. They blasted Haitian music, waved Haitian flags, and turned shame into pride sending a message: being Haitian was nothing to be ashamed of.

For my parents, though, the violence was proof that danger was everywhere. To them, every Haitian gathering looked like trouble waiting to happen. They doubled down on their rules and forbade us from going to Haitian parties or hanging out with groups of them, especially at night, to avoid any violent confrontations with other non-Haitian groups known as "bals." There were many of them, and I desperately wanted to go. I loved to dance and longed to embrace Haitian culture fully, especially now that I lived in Miami where Haitians were everywhere, unlike in Paris. But full access to the culture was off-limits during those volatile years. Around then,

Michel Martelly, better known as Sweet Micky, was the king of konpa. His songs were filled with sexual innuendo and vulgarity, the kind of lyrics my father, a pastor, would never have allowed. So instead, I joined the Haitian dance team at school, which performed to more permissible traditional hits. My parents encouraged that. They supported any cultural expression that felt "old school Haitian," but they rejected anything that strayed from what they considered old-school, traditional, proper music. Any variation outside of that was dismissed as vagabond nonsense. For boys, vagabond meant blasting vulgar rap like "2 Live Crew", objectifying women, wearing pants without a belt so their boxers showed, swapping proper church shoes for sneakers, or growing long dreads. Girls could also be branded vagabonds, with their gold teeth, bamboo earrings, tight clothes, and salt-and-pepper asymmetrical haircuts. It was an embodiment of loud styles that, to our parents, looked like rebellion rather than respectability. Still, even with all the warnings, I couldn't help but experiment with some of those styles I saw in the rap videos, trying to fit in despite their disapproval. Being one of five girls also meant my parents couldn't afford professional styling for all of us on a regular basis. So, I learned how to braid hair on my own. I started with my sisters' hair, then I learned to do my own. Word spread, and soon neighbors asked me to braid theirs. Even kids from school came to me. Braiding became a side hustle that made me valuable. Maybe it was my subconscious way of finding my place after those months in Allapattah when I had felt so worthless.

 My parents wanted to uphold what they saw as the good old Haitian days. To me, when I was young, it felt like hypocrisy. In France, they had assimilated well, but in Miami, they seemed to want to rewind the clock all the way back to their youth in Haiti. On one hand, they encouraged me to exude Haitian pride by entering Haitian community programs like the Miss Haiti South Florida pageant, which I won. On the other hand, because of the stigma and violence surrounding Haitian kids in Miami, everyone I introduced to them was labeled a vagabond. That left me living a double life, blending in with kids at school while maintaining a stricter Haitian image at home.

There was even a time when my father decided his daughters couldn't wear pants anymore and had to wear loose ankle-length skirts. I used to hide jeans in my backpack and change the minute I left the house. In any case, that dress code didn't last long, especially after we girls revolted and my mother's charm helped ease the tension. In the midst of these confusing mixed signals, I started to rebel. And the first order of rebellion was boys. I only had two boyfriends before marrying Russell, and they were both Haitian. They were what you would call "bad boys." Not studious. They had swagger, the kind of boys who skipped class, sagged their pants low, carried themselves like they were untouchable; they were the kind of boys teachers warned you about and parents prayed you'd avoid.

My first boyfriend, "M," and I met in junior high. He was new to our school after moving from New York. He was quiet, with that Brooklyn street-style swagger that made him mysterious. We were together for two years. It was an innocent relationship, only alive during school hours and on the phone. We never hung out after school or on weekends because of my strict parents. The one time I agreed to skip school with him, we had sex. We were in ninth grade. It was painful, awkward, and forgettable, the kind of thing that happens when kids think they're in love but don't know what they're doing. After that, maybe I skipped a handful more times to be with him, but that was it. When the school year ended, so did we. It felt natural. My next boyfriend, "R," was two grades ahead of me; he was a senior and I was just a freshman. He smoked weed, I didn't. He was affiliated with the Zoe Pound gang, something I gathered by observation. I think I liked the thrill because my parents forbade me to be around that type. He was popular in school, a basketball player whose future was saved by the sport. Basketball pulled him away from bad influences. His ex-girlfriend was still obsessed with him and tried to pick fights with me in the hallway. He would protect me every time, but eventually it got too crazy. I was an honor student, and she wasn't worth the trouble. Plus at the beginning of the next year, when I moved up to 11th grade, we broke up. He left to play ball at a community college and let's just say I knew he wouldn't stay faithful.

To be clear, I wasn't scared of his ex-girlfriend and I wasn't a punk either. From time to time I wore Dickie suits like my brother, and carried myself with a hint of a tomboyish swagger, though always with a feminine twist. My brother taught me how to defend myself, and I only ever got into one real physical fight. It was with a girl named Sandra, who was, at the time, a friend of mine. I happened to lend her my pair of Nike Cortez sneakers and after some time, asked for them back. To my surprise, she refused, acting like she deserved to keep them, as if the shoes were owed to her. Looking back, I can't help but wonder if part of that entitlement came from the Haitian stigma prominent at the time. It felt as though giving them back wasn't necessary because I was Haitian. One day she showed up at my house with a group of other kids, taunting and daring me to take the shoes back. Well, let's just say I did what needed to be done. My poor grandmother stood at the front door, not knowing what to do, shouting "Anmwe!" (pronounced "ahn-mway"), a Creole expression used to cry out in shock or alarm similar to the way you might yell "Oh my God!" or "Oh no!" I had never seen her so animated, but after it was over, I walked back inside with my Nikes in tow, closed the door, and called it a day. I've never had another fight since. It was degrading, beneath me, and beneath my family's name. That was the moment I realized exactly what my parents were trying to protect me from.

My mother hated both of my boyfriends, not because they were Haitian, but because to her, they symbolized distraction and wasted potential. She and my father had sacrificed too much for us to become stagnant with all the progress we had made. Settling for anyone who didn't aspire to grow at the same vibration as our family was unacceptable. At the time, I thought she was judgmental, maybe even harsh, but I now understand she was simply afraid. She had lived and seen too much. She was trying to protect me from detours that could have cost me everything. We weren't being raised casually; we were being trained. Not in a gym. Not in a classroom. But in a pressure cooker of performance, pride, and past wounds. We were being trained to excel in a world that would never slow down for us. That training became part of my wiring. Even now, when people ask where my drive comes from, they don't realize that it wasn't initially from ambition, it was from survival.

My mom built a fortress around her home, her children, and her identity. She tried to perfect everything she could touch. That was her armor. That was how she fought back, and it became the beginning of a trickle-down effect. She fought to become the best, and when you've achieved what she and my father had achieved in France in such a short time, you could understand why she would never settle. The finish line was always moving, and every time we reached it, it reset. There was no room for mistakes, no cushion for mediocrity. Just an undercurrent that told us to do more, be more, and go further.

But along with that drive came something else, something I now call a subtle kind of sadism, though I don't think it was intentional. It showed up in comparison. "Your sister got into this Ivy League college, make sure you keep your grades up to be able to do the same." Or "Look, Dr. X's daughter is going to become a doctor." The message was indirect, but it landed hard: Maybe my mom thought she was motivating us. But over time, it created unspoken competition and quiet resentment between siblings. I don't believe it came from malice. I think it came from what she knew. My mother had spent her childhood competing in boarding school for space, approval, and love. For her, survival meant outperforming.

That mindset was passed down to us, not as punishment but as preparation. Their unfinished dreams became the gasoline for ours. We weren't just encouraged to succeed; we were propelled to.

School became another stage for me to prove myself. I joined every extracurricular activity that I could; Haitian dance club, basketball, track, and even volleyball. Volleyball became my love; I was really good at it. I could have been great at basketball too, but the one day a girl from Central High School scratched my face, I said to myself, "Oh no, not the face!" and gave it up quicker than a New Year's resolution. Volleyball, however, was the path that allowed me to earn a college scholarship at St. Thomas University. High school is where I came into my own. I was in the student government, and voted in as the school secretary. I was accepted into the prestigious International Baccalaureate (IB) program and graduated ranked 43rd in my class, which wasn't bad for a girl who had arrived at age nine not speaking a word of English. High school was my training ground, and I didn't even know it. But more than anything, it was the place where I rediscovered my confidence and started to command space again.

In hindsight, there was no blueprint for balance in our home, there were only blueprints for greatness. Even when no one said it out loud, the message was clear: strive higher, do better, be the best. Excellence wasn't optional. It was the baseline. That kind of wiring doesn't happen overnight. It's embedded early, in the way you're spoken to, the way you're corrected, the way expectations are set before you even understand them. It becomes instinct. In our household, there was always something to do and always something to improve. With seven kids, attention was earned. You didn't get praised for doing well because you were expected to do well. And if you didn't? You fixed it. Fast. That was the standard. Discipline, hard work, and performance weren't just encouraged, they were demanded. I didn't just inherit their expectations, I inherited their unfinished business, and for years, that business became my mission. I believed my path was only about proving myself, chasing standards I didn't set, and carrying a weight that was never fully mine. But then my world cracked open the minute I met Russell.

GUERDY OVER THE YEARS GROWING UP IN MIAMI

Chapter 6
FINDING "MY RUSSELL"

The way we met wasn't cinematic, it was just a regular after-school girls' volleyball practice in the gym during 10th grade. My teammates and I were mid-drill when our head volleyball coach suddenly walked in with a handful of guys from the basketball team. I recognized a few of them as teammates of RP, who was my boyfriend at the time. For a second, I wondered if we had mixed up the schedule and the boys were there for their timeslot. But then the coach explained he had recruited some of the basketball guys to help launch a boys' volleyball program. Russell was one of them. That was the first time we had direct contact.

Coach wanted us to start helping them learn the basic skills, and so we did. But when the coach briefly stepped out of the gym, some of us started goofing around, lining up to take turns at spiking drills just for fun. Russell grabbed a volleyball and began using it like a basketball, dribbling and shooting it at the hoop. I joined in too, since I had played basketball before.

I had seen Russell before, but we'd never interacted. I saw him, but I didn't really see him. In fact, he and RP were teammates on the basketball team. They weren't good friends since Russell was a freshman on the team, but they weren't strangers either. RP's youngest sister was best friends with Russell's youngest sister, and my own sister was friends with Russell's older sister. Around that same time, my family moved out of the first house we had lived in when we came to Miami and into a neighborhood closer to Russell. That proximity became its own kind of destiny.

It wasn't until my relationship with RP ended that Russell began to show up differently, or maybe it was me who finally had the space to notice him. It was the beginning of our Senior year when I'd pass him in the hall and say "Hi," but his reply was so soft-spoken that I thought he wasn't answering me at all. The second time was the same, and I finally confronted him: "When someone says hi, the polite thing is to say hi back." He smiled and explained that he *had* said hi, but I probably hadn't heard him, that was the misunderstanding. By the third time, he skipped the awkward greeting altogether and went straight in for a hug. That hug changed everything. It wasn't romantic so much as it was grounding. Like I had been moving too fast for too long, and suddenly someone offered me stillness. Russell didn't flirt, he didn't chase, he didn't put on a show. He just stood there, solid and aware. That was who he was from the very beginning. At first, it was like destiny was nudging us together in quiet ways. The more it happened, the more it felt orchestrated; like life itself was determined to weave us together. I'd pop into the counselor's office on a whim, and there he was. I'd head to the library, and he'd be sitting at a table. I'd duck into a teacher's classroom at lunch to pass the time, and somehow, he'd wander in too. High school had a hundred places to disappear, yet we always ended up in the same room. We started to hang out together a lot.

By then, people were starting to ask us if we were together. One day, half-serious and half-joking, I turned to him and said, "Everyone keeps asking what we are… so what do we say?" In his typical simple, clever way, he looked at me and said, "If it walks like a duck and talks like a duck, then it's a duck." That was Russell's way of making it official, and just like that, we were boyfriend and girlfriend. There was no grand gesture, no drama, just clarity and certainty.

But once Russell and I became official, I could sense the shift. I knew a few girls had crushes on him before me, and once we were together, their vibe toward me changed. Some pulled back and some gave side-eyes, it was subtle, but obvious. And it wasn't the only time I felt that kind of jealousy. When I was voted into student government as secretary, a few of the other nominees weren't as friendly anymore. Later, when I was crowned prom queen, what should have been pure celebration carried the same undertones of envy, with some girls distancing themselves again. Whether it was my relationship or my wins, the pattern was the same.

But through all of that noise, Russell never wavered. He didn't feed into the drama and didn't get caught up in popularity contests. He stayed the same; steady, grounded, protective. Russell is a Scorpio; quiet, private, intuitive, and observant in a way that makes you feel both studied and safe. He never spoke to fill space; when he spoke, it was intentional. He wasn't shy, but more so selective in his expressions. And that kind of selectiveness made him magnetic. Fortunately for me, he wasn't trying to charm just anyone, he wanted me. I, on the other hand, am a Capricorn; structured, ambitious, relentless, always with a plan. Where he moved by instinct, I moved by design or like Earth and water. Opposites in many ways, yet twin flames nonetheless.

But even in his calm, confident way, there was one night early in our relationship where the intensity of his feelings for me cracked through. Prom. We were both nominated for king and queen, and while I took the crown, Russell didn't. His childhood friend Mike did. It was the first time I had ever seen him truly upset, even jealous. Standing there with my crown, taking photos with Mike, I could feel it radiating off of him. We had planned to go to a nice restaurant afterward, but Russell didn't want to go anymore. He drove us straight home. His mood was heavy. The night was ruined in one sense, but in another, it was unforgettable. Because that was the first and only time his guard slipped, showing me that when it came to me, he didn't play. It wasn't petty jealousy, it was love, raw and unfiltered and I secretly loved every minute of it.

There was something about my relationship with Russell that was totally different from my two previous ones. Those relationships had been rushed, and surface level only. Russell erased them from my memory. To this day, the thing that still amazes me is that I was his one and only. There were no other girls before me. And yes, he was obviously different from me. He was white with English, Italian, and Cuban roots, while I was Black with Haitian Caribbean roots, but somehow it didn't feel awkward to be with each other. I had grown up in France, surrounded by a cultural and racial mix, so being with someone from a different background felt familiar to me. He had grown up in the same neighborhood that shifted over time, becoming more diverse. They leaned into their community, never making race a wedge. That was part of why being together felt so seamless. He wasn't trying to be a wannabe or cool for his basketball friends by dating a Black girl, and it wasn't about crossing cultures as some kind of novelty; that was perhaps one of the many reasons why being together felt so effortless.

Once we were official, the next step was meeting each other's parents. When Russell met mine, there was already a built-in comfort; our sisters were friends, which softened the introduction.

The first meeting was smooth, and from there, my parents quickly began to understand why I was so drawn to him. They noticed the changes in me, I was calmer and more grounded. With Russell, I could sit in silence without fidgeting. He read rooms the way I didn't yet know how, pointing out things I couldn't see and protecting me in subtle ways. My parents saw that and respected it.

Everybody loved Russell when they met him. He had an aura that made people lean in; he was calm, almost angelic. People sometimes mistook his quietness for shyness, but it wasn't that, he was reserved and observant, similar to my father, in fact, a fellow Scorpio.

And the same was true when I met his parents. Integrating into his family was seamless. Russell's father, Steve, was sarcastic, brilliant, and commanding. He was the fixer of his family. The kind of man who didn't say "I love you," but showed up when you needed him. First came the complaints; the grumbling under his breath, the eye rolls, the act like he was carrying the weight of the world. But then came the solutions. Jill, his youngest daughter, got pregnant at a young age. Angie, the oldest, was smart, sharp, destined to be the engineer she eventually became, but she always seemed to end up in a fender bender. And Russell, he didn't give his dad much trouble at all. If anything, he was lucky to have Steve to look up to, and Steve respected the way Russell carried himself. No matter what the situation, Steve might complain, but he'd always handle it; helping Jill face her new reality, getting Angie back on the road, or helping Russell at a young age set up his neighborhood lawn-mowing business. That was his love language: action; and, in his own way, acceptance. Russell mirrored his father in many ways. Both Scorpios, they shared the same protective streak and the same instinct to show up when it mattered most. Their leadership looked different. Steve was outward, commanding, quick to bark and quick to fix; Russell was quiet, steady, measured. But the baseline was the same: if you were theirs, you were covered.

Steve and I had a relationship built on that sarcasm. I liked it. I matched it. I got it. He respected that I was a leader too. Short and sweet. Straight to the point. We didn't need to butter each other up, we just needed to get things done. He would pop kiss me on the lips like with his kids once in a while when we greeted or said goodbye. It never felt strange, I was part of the family. His way reminded me of my grandmother in many ways. She wasn't overly emotional, she didn't smother you with affection, but when it came, it mattered. Quality over quantity. That was how I read Steve, and it was why I liked him from the beginning.

His mother, Florence, "ObiFlo", as the kids eventually nicknamed her, was the opposite energy. She was patient where he was quick, gentle where he was commanding. She had been thrust into womanhood early: her mother died when Florence was just 16, leaving her the only girl in a house with her father and three brothers. Duty became her survival, not her choice. From that point on, she became the homemaker, keeping everything running with quiet grace. Folding towels like it was an art form. Setting tables with precision. Cooking with effortless skill. She didn't do it for applause; it was simply what had to be done, and in the process, she became extraordinary at it.

Florence also had this cool, understated vibe. With her platinum or sometimes red-dyed hair, she always carried the look of the lead singer of The Cranberries without even trying. She could blend into any conversation with ease, well-read enough that you'd never guess how abruptly her girlhood had ended. She was witty, soft-spoken, and always on the nose when she did chime in, very much like Russell. That balance of warmth and subtle sharpness made her magnetic in her own quiet way.

Her nickname, ObiFlo, said it all. The boys gave it to her as a mash-up of Obi-Wan Kenobi, the wise Jedi who mentored Luke Skywalker from Russell's favorite movie, *Star Wars*. It stuck because it fit. She had that mystical, steady wisdom you couldn't quite pin down, but you felt it. She was their north star, the anchor in their house.

At first, Florence wasn't ecstatic about me stepping into Russell's world. He was her only son, her best friend, and sharing him wasn't easy. But over time, she saw that I wasn't taking him away, I was adding to their circle. Slowly, our bond grew. Eventually, it became so strong that we now have a group chat called "Trio," just me, Russell, and her, where we talk every day about the most ordinary, silly things. She became not just my mother-in-law, but my friend.

Their home was the backdrop of their legacy. Russell and his sisters had been born in that house, and the family had stayed there through every wave of change in the neighborhood. Even as demographics shifted, they didn't leave. They leaned into the community. Years later, after Steve took the fire chief position in Dallas and his parents moved, Russell and I were excited to buy the house. To outsiders it might have looked like just a piece of real estate, but to us it was continuity. Proof of how deeply we were rooted not just in each other, but in the community that had shaped us. We kept the house for years. Miles, our first son, was even born while we lived there. Eventually, when the neighborhood began to deteriorate when the 2008 real estate crash hit, we made the choice to sell. But that house will always mean more to us than a line on a deed, it was where our family story deepened.

The Abrairas helped me adapt to American culture in ways that were surprisingly fun. I'll never forget one dinner when Florence had made jambalaya rice. I smiled and said, "I love CA-JOON food." Everyone froze, then burst out laughing. They gently corrected me, it's Cajun. Another time, I pronounced "television" the French way: *teh-leh-vee-zyon*. More laughter. It was never cruel, it was endearing. Through them, I wasn't just learning language, I was learning how to laugh at myself and how to belong.

That distinction mattered. French tonality and humor are so different from American ones. In France, voices drop at the end of sentences, matter-of-fact and blunt. In the U.S., voices rise, everything ending on a high note, more sing-song. My naturally low voice, paired with that French cadence, often made me sound cold or even rude without meaning to. That "rude French" stigma followed me into adulthood; even into The Real Housewives of Miami years later where my tone was often misread. But in Russell's family, especially with Steve, that bluntness was understood. He and I spoke the same way, direct, no frills; and that connection made me feel at home right away.

When we first got together, we were shocked to find out that we lived only a few blocks apart. A minute or two in a car, or about ten minutes walking. Russell would make us sandwiches for school, and sometimes his mom would let him borrow her brand new Mazda to pick me up to go to school. That foundation of small acts of service became the heartbeat of our love. He would even help me take out my braids which was hours of work, but never complained. That kind of patience, that kind of willingness to do something he didn't understand just because it mattered to me, that was Russell. We even faced a brief pregnancy scare in high school. This is the first time I've ever shared this. I immediately thought about having an abortion because of the Réjouis Rule: fix the problem, move on. I wanted to abort; he wanted to talk about keeping it. That moment tested us, but it also revealed the depth of our bond. That's when I knew he was ride-or-die.

By senior year, I found myself at a crossroads. I had fallen in love with Latin ballroom dancing, a love sparked by watching the movie *Dance With Me,* and I had been taking salsa lessons, convinced maybe this was my calling. I dreamed of moving to New York City and pursuing ballroom dancing while attending NYU. New York had always pulled at me, reminding me of the cosmopolitan rhythm I had once known in France. The energy, the pace, and the feeling of belonging to a global city, echoed the life I had before Miami.

One night, sitting in the car with Russell, we faced it head-on: would I go to New York to chase this dream, and try to keep us alive long-distance, knowing it would probably fail? Or would I stay, root myself here, and build a life with him? The answer came as soon as our eyes met. We both knew I wasn't going anywhere. I stayed. And it was the best decision I've ever made. Sitting in that car, I knew Russell was my destiny. The certainty of him was undeniable. But certainty doesn't erase the voice of upbringing. The Réjouis rules were still in the back of my head, whispering that greatness meant chasing the biggest, boldest dream, even if it meant leaving love behind.

For me, that meant New York, NYU, ballroom dancing and a chance to step into a life that felt more like Paris than Miami. So, I sat there with two truths pressed against each other: the woman who had found forever, and the girl still programmed to believe that success meant climbing higher, no matter the cost. Choosing Russell didn't mean I lacked ambition. It meant I was learning, for the first time, that success could look like love, like partnership, like building something together. That night, I quietly rewrote the Rulebook. My parents, for their part, had probably imagined me matching my siblings'

Ivy League paths and enrolling somewhere prestigious to make their sacrifices feel justified. But, by the time high school ended, they could already see that Russell and I were serious. When I chose to stay in Miami instead of pursuing ballroom and NYU, that was the moment they realized I wasn't going to follow the Ivy League track. They accepted it. They had seen my confidence strengthen through the fire of every transition and every test. After all, I had survived when the odds were stacked against me, they knew Guerdy would be okay. I wasn't the fragile one. I had charisma, grit, and the ability to make my way in any room. So, when Russell asked my father for his blessing, they didn't resist. They trusted that I had chosen right.

Once I decided to stay in Miami for university, to keep us together, it was smooth sailing from there. Our future was locked in. After we graduated high school, we both attended St. Thomas University. I received a volleyball Scholarship and Russell a basketball scholarship. They weren't full rides, but alluring enough to go. My other siblings had gone off to Ivy League schools, and me going to NYU might have been great for my parents, but after meeting Russell, I eased up on trying to cross an invisible line that always seemed to keep moving. I was no longer constantly chasing approval from my parents to maintain the Réjouis standard among my siblings. He taught me there was more to life than just this programming of pursuing perfection at all costs.

I adapted to that, yet still had that Réjouis handbook stored in the back of my mind, which would resurface later in my life. Russell enrolled in sports administration. He initially aspired to work in some capacity in college or pro sports. But eventually, during our final year in college, he decided that the heavy networking, or as he described it, "ass kissing" was not for him. He wanted no part of it. "That world's not for me," he told me. Instead, after graduating with a degree in sports administration, he followed his lineage. His father, grandfather, and two of his uncles were all firefighters. It was in his blood. He said it like it was inevitable. "I'm not trying to be something I'm not. This is what I'm meant to do." And he did it; with humility, with courage, and with his usual quiet confidence.

His proposal reflected exactly who he was: simple, clear, and true. One night on the beach, just the two of us, he got down on one knee and asked me to marry him. When Russell proposed, I didn't hesitate. It was an easy yes. Not because it was perfect like the movies, but because I had already tested us. At one point, I broke up with him, convinced that love was supposed to look like the fairy tales my mother idolized during her Princess Diana era: flowers, daily compliments, and dramatic declarations. Another reason was fear. I worried that because I was his one and only, he might grow tired of me one day. I even told him he should "explore" if he ever felt the need. He shut that down immediately, looking me dead in the eyes and saying, "Don't ever say that again. I don't want anyone else." To Russell, that breakup wasn't even real, it was just a hiccup. He knew all along that I'd come back once I realized what we had was rare; and he was right. Less than a month later, I returned, and this time I understood. Why chase after illusions when reality was this good? I had a man I was madly in love with. He was extremely attractive, sexy, loyal, unwavering, faithful and caring. He was my home, my anchor, and the calm I never knew I needed. Part of what reassured me was knowing we weren't stepping into love blindly. Both of our parents had modeled what lasting commitment looked like. They didn't come into their marriages with long lists of partners before them; they recognized "the one," chose, and built lives that endured for decades. Russell and I were cut from that same cloth. There was a quiet beauty in realizing that what we had wasn't fragile; it was rooted, generational and steady.

So, when he got down on one knee, the setting couldn't have been more us.

After a simple dinner at Macaroni Grill, he suggested that we go for a walk on the Beach. We didn't do that often, but we would on occasions when we had things to discuss in private or just wanted to relax. He asked me to marry him with the ocean as our witness.

Before I even answered, my first words were, "Did you ask my dad?" That was the Réjouis way, nothing happened without his approval; and yes, Russell had already gone to him and did it the same way he did everything else, calmly, respectfully, and directly. There was no big speech, no theatrics. Just man-to-man clarity. My dad respected that. It showed him that Russell wasn't about show, he was about substance.

Because of the certainty we felt for each other, we didn't rush into each phase of our lives. By the time he proposed, we had already been together six years, and our engagement lasted another year and a half, not because of hesitation, but because we knew we were forever. We got married at 25.

Our love was steady so we were intentional with taking our time and our decision to build our family. I was 30 years old when Miles was born, and six years later Liam came along. With Russell, there was never a rush. We trusted the timing of our lives and it worked out in our favor.

There's something about choosing a career like firefighting: it isn't for everyone. When everyone else is running out of the fire and away from danger, they're the brave ones who run in.

That level of devotion and heroic selflessness, can't really be explained.

Russell had no ego, no need to compete with me and no hesitation in stepping into whatever role our family needed. His firefighter schedule was 24 hours on and 48 hours off. This unique schedule actually made it possible for me to advance my career the way I did. He was willingly present at home, handling school pick-ups, bedtime routines, laundry, and the everyday grind. Other times, in between his shifts and family responsibilities, he would help at my warehouses, bring set up equipment and decor to events, and even make flower deliveries. He never made me feel guilty or resented me for my drive to build something that seemed unimaginable at the time. He supported both home and business with the same steady hands. Both of us had grown up watching marriages that lasted so we weren't strangers to commitment, endurance, or choosing one person and staying the course. That was the blueprint we inherited, and it became the one we carried forward. With that kind of foundation beneath us, anything felt possible. It was the steady ground on which we would build the next chapter of our lives; one that would test not only our union, but also the resilience that had been woven into us long before we ever met.

GUERDY & RUSSELL, HIGH SCHOOL

GUERDY & RUSSELL'S BABY SHOWER ON FISHER ISLAND, 2007

RUSSELL WITH HIS AND GUERDY'S PARENTS

Finding "My Russell"

RUSSELL WITH HIS PARENTS AND SISTERS

**OUR FAMILY TRIP TO JAPAN AS
MILES' HIGH SCHOOL GRADUATION GIFT, 2025**

Chapter 7

A PLANNER IN THE MAKING

Work was the heartbeat of the Réjouis household. In a family of seven children, no one got by on charm or excuses. You pulled your own weight, self-sufficiency wasn't optional, it was the mandate. By thirteen, I had already followed in the footsteps of my sisters, working for a family friend named Louis at his mortgage and real estate office. In Miami's Haitian community, being resourceful meant survival and opportunities were passed around by word of mouth with one hand helping the other. Each of my sisters had worked for him at one point or another. It was never a full-time thing due to school, just a part-time job on Saturdays that gave us pocket money and experience. It became a family tradition; when one sister graduated and left for college, the next one in line would take her place at Louis's office.

Those Saturdays working for Louis carried its own ritual. We could count on two things: first, Louis would arrive in the morning with a box of warm Krispy Kreme donuts for breakfast, and second, by lunchtime, he would order takeout. Takeout was usually legume, my favorite Haitian meal. Those two things were a guarantee, week after week, and I always looked forward to it since it was pretty much the only time I got to eat food from outside the house. We didn't go out to restaurants unless it was a major event like graduation. Even birthdays were celebrated at home, marked with a meal and a cake baked by one of our neighbors who sold pastries out of her house.

Louis was extremely generous. Aside from the hourly pay, he would always give me an extra couple of bucks just because. He was like an uncle. He never stayed in the office for long, as working in real estate basically turned his car into a mobile office. He was always running from meeting to meeting and most of the time, he'd be in the building for no more than an hour; just long enough to grab files, sign some things, and dash back out. Every time, you'd hear him repeating, "I've got to go, I've got to go, I've got to go," like a broken record. I always used to rush out behind him with paperwork, trying to catch him before he disappeared into his car and sped away to his next appointment. He was funny without even knowing it. His pants were always a little disheveled, his shirt sleeves rolled up, and he gave off this air of being slightly aloof, but clearly, he wasn't, because his business was thriving.

For the first time, I felt like I was redeeming myself from those earlier experiences, from sitting helplessly on the lobby floor beside my grandmother, to the silent isolation of that Allapattah house where the language barrier kept me on the outside. Without knowing it, Louis was helping me. By leaving me in a room full of paperwork and ringing phones, he forced me to be the adult in the room which gave me confidence, and helped shape me back into that girl who once stood on her teacher's desk in France, telling the class what to do. Louis's little office was the beginning of the beginning for me. It was the seed. It wasn't in full bloom yet, but it planted something vital within me; the sense that I could be needed, trusted, and in control. Later, in college, working for him on weekends and pushing myself further, I began to grow into that voice fully.

When we attended college, Russell and I both lived at home. He had the car so we commuted together to St. Thomas University, balancing classes, work and practices since we were also both playing sports. I played volleyball, and Russell played basketball. St. Thomas was local so we already knew some of the students on campus from playing against them in high school. The transition felt seamless. I was majoring in Communication Arts, a field that allowed me to combine creativity, organization, and storytelling in a way that felt natural to me. It would later become the foundation for how I built my brand.

By my sophomore year, though, the pull for independence grew stronger. Living at home was wearing me down. My parents, with the best intentions, kept leaning on Russell and me for help. My mom, bless her, was the worst driver on the planet, and somehow Russell became her go-to chauffeur. If it ever started raining, she would literally stop her car in the middle of the road, leave it stranded, and call Russell to come rescue her. She wouldn't even pull-over to the side, she would just brake, park, and wait. To this day, I've never met anyone who had rain trauma like that.

On top of that, I had a younger sister who was nine years younger than me. I became the built-in babysitter. If I wasn't watching her, I was taking her to extracurriculars, or Russell was. We joked that we had become mini-parents without ever signing up for it. Between babysitting duties, family errands, and constant requests, Russell and I rarely had time alone, and intimacy was slipping through the cracks. Things had to change so I finally made a bold decision; I wanted independence. Even though St. Thomas was only twenty minutes away, I took out a loan so that I could live on campus. It wasn't the practical choice, but for my growth, it was the only choice. For the first time, I had my own space. I was finally free from constant family obligations, and even though it came at a cost, the freedom was worth every dollar.

I applied for and landed one of the most coveted positions on campus: the role of Resident Assistant (RA). The job came with perks; not just free housing, but a suite. While most students were packed into single rooms and forced to use the community bathrooms down the hall, my RA suite came with its own kitchen, private bathroom, and shower. That was the life. Everyone wanted that setup, and I had earned it. As an RA, I was responsible for monitoring students in the dorms and doing rounds with another RA. Walking the halls, checking for noise complaints, and enforcing rules wasn't glamorous, but it taught me a new kind of authority. It was on one of those rounds that I first smelled weed. Russell and I had never smoked, so I had no idea what the odor was. It wasn't until another RA told me, "That's weed," that I even realized what I was smelling. That moment wasn't about the weed itself; it was about me stepping out of the bubble I had been raised in. My parents had sheltered me so much. I had never been to parties and had no real social exposure. Now I was finally learning about the world in real time, one discovery at a time. Of course, I wasn't a perfect enforcer. I bent the rules when my heart got involved. I snuck Russell into my suite and he was a fixture there, even though it was against policy. The irony wasn't lost on me; the RA breaking the very rules I was supposed to uphold. But love doesn't care about policies.

Beyond RA life, I was at the center of campus involvement. I became president of TV45, the university television station, where

I managed programming, schedules, and an entire crew of students with their own strong opinions. It was creativity and crisis management rolled into one, and it gave me my first taste of running a production that demanded vision and leadership. Beyond that, I threw myself into clubs and organizations, staying involved in everything I could. By then my plate was overflowing: sports, TV45, RA duties, classes, clubs, Russell, babysitting, and part-time jobs. But somehow, in the overflow, I thrived. I wasn't just present at St. Thomas, I was everywhere. If something was happening on campus, chances are, I was in the middle of it.

By my junior year, I needed to start building up internship hours to graduate, so, I picked up work at the university alumni office, helping a few times a week with mailouts and basic clerical work. On top of that, I also needed money, since I had stopped working for Louis at the mortgage office. That's when I landed a receptionist job at a pool construction company in North Miami. The pool company was nothing glamorous but for me, it was another stepping stone toward independence. I sat at the front desk, answering phones, filing paperwork and greeting clients. From the start, I approached it with the same determination I had brought everywhere else. When I first interviewed, they asked if I had a car. I didn't have a car yet, but I said yes, knowing that if I got the job, I'd make it happen; and I did. The very same day, Russell, his dad, and I went out and bought a white Nissan Sentra. It wasn't a lie, just a matter of sequence. I wasn't going to let something like transportation stand in the way of an opportunity.

Before long, the company cleared out a room and turned it into a marketing office just for me. By senior year, as my schedule lightened, I was splitting time between the alumni office and the pool company. Volleyball no longer fit. The team's travel schedule cut into work, so I gave up my partial scholarship and paid the rest of my tuition myself. My RA position already covered housing and meals, so the money I earned went to car payments, living expenses, and savings. Russell also stepped back from basketball, focusing on his classes and working in the university mailroom.

That year, the pool company offered me a part-time marketing job, and after graduation it became full-time. The role didn't even exist before me. It was created specifically because they wanted me to stay. I had made such an impact that they didn't want to lose me. They were expanding into pavers, with a new warehouse and sales office, and trusted me to help shape the brand. The $25,000 salary felt like big bucks back then and the income was steady. I had earned it on my own and it was proof that I could create momentum on my own.

However, even after graduation, I stayed closely connected to St. Thomas. I often volunteered for special occasions and was still very present on campus. Surprisingly, that visibility led to an unexpected offer; a full-time position in the Alumni Relations Office, which I accepted. The university itself had a unique Catholic history. Originally an all-male school, its traditions and donor base still carried traces of that past. Stepping into that environment as a young woman meant learning to navigate a very particular culture, and it became part of my education just as much as my coursework had been.

On paper, the job looked far more glamorous than it really was. What jumped out at me were the luncheons and special events hosted for alumni. That side of it seemed fun, spontaneous, and exciting. No two days were alike. It provided me with a chance to be creative and social all at once.

In reality, most of the work was far less shiny. My days were filled with paperwork, call logs, mail-outs, and endless meetings. The core of the job was fundraising. I hated that part because I dreaded asking people for money. It tugged directly at my control issues. That sense of dependence, of waiting for someone else to say yes, went against everything I had built to protect myself. And those "yeses" didn't come easily. Relationships had to be cultivated. I learned quickly that people gave to people they liked and trusted. That was the key, earning trust and connection. It took time, it took grace, and it required a kind of patience I hadn't practiced before.

The fundraising side of the role came with its own learning curve, too. I often found myself at luncheons or dinners seated across from much older male alumni, making polite conversation and asking for donations. In hindsight, I sometimes wonder what the optics must have been like, me, all dressed up, leaning across a table with an older gentleman. I can only imagine what people may have thought.

Little did I know, though, that this was training for the exact same dynamic I'd face later in my career; sitting across from the father of the bride, persuading him to upgrade the bar to super-premium. Those moments gave me a unique fearlessness; an ability to walk into any room and connect, and to hold my own with anyone, regardless of age, creed, class, or background. What kept me motivated was the event-planning side of the role. Whenever there was a luncheon or special gathering to coordinate, I lit up. One event in particular at Bal Harbour put me in the right place at the right time. It was there I met Ted Johnson. That introduction changed everything, setting me on the path toward my real calling.

I was hosting my first alumni soirée at a hotel in Bal Harbour, where the catering director, Ted, and I worked closely on the logistics. He noticed how quickly I could size up the room, sort out the layout, and make fast decisions. He complimented me, saying I was really good at party planning, and I took note of that. As we continued working together, he told me he was about to transfer to the Radisson in downtown Miami to build a new catering team. "I want people who can sell ice to an Eskimo," he joked, and then added that he'd love for me to join him.

By that point, I had been at the alumni office for about a year and a half. In hindsight, it was a relatively short time, but if I counted my internship and volunteer work, I had already been connected to that department much longer. Still, it didn't feel right anymore. I wasn't happy with the constant cycle of alumni lunches and meetings where, at the core, my role was to ask for money. It was tied to fundraising, which leaned heavily on the nonprofit corporate side of things. That wasn't where my energy lived.

What made it clearer was the contrast I felt inside myself. There was always a different pep in my step when I was planning an event compared to when I was heading to yet another one-on-one lunch for an ask. Event planning lit me up; fundraising weighed me down. The Radisson, on the other hand, felt like a chance to do what came naturally to me. It was still social, but without the weight of asking for donations. It was about creating experiences, working with people face-to-face, and delivering something they were excited to invest in; not convincing them to give out of obligation. For me, that was a huge difference. Everything in life happens for a reason, and I saw this opportunity as exactly that.

Walking into the Radisson in downtown Miami was like walking into another universe. Gone were the quiet corridors of the alumni office, where I lived in paperwork and donor lists. Here, the lobby buzzed with energy, and the moment I joined Ted's team, I knew I had entered an entirely new arena. Ted threw me into the deep end quickly, and I wasn't about to sink. He insisted I rotate through every department to understand how the hotel operated from the inside out. I wasn't just learning catering; I was shadowing sales, banquets, accounting, and even spending time in the kitchen, where I helped plate dishes so I could see firsthand how long it took to put out each course. Some days I was front of the house, in heels with clients in ballrooms; other days I was back of the house, in flats, learning the mechanics that made service flow. I learned how each department had its own rhythm and politics, and how none of them worked in isolation. If one team dropped the ball, the entire operation suffered.

As a catering manager, I was taught early that my word was gospel once it went into a Banquet Event Order. A banquet event order (BEO) is the document that spells out every single detail of an event, from the exact number of chairs to the tablecloth color, to the entrée timing, even to the type of wine being poured. Once it was signed off, the entire hotel staff followed it like a script. If I missed a detail, it wasn't just my mistake; dozens of people would follow the wrong plan, and the entire event could collapse. That weight forced precision into me. It was no longer about looking polished or schmoozing. It was about commanding logistics down to the inch, and if I didn't know the answer, I learned to get one fast.

My first wedding at the Radisson sealed it for me. It wasn't even in one of the ballrooms, it was set outside by the pool. The bride and groom stood at the top of a paved staircase that overlooked the water, framed like a vision, while all the guests waited below, craning their necks to watch them descend. I can still see her face when she stepped forward, her gasp, her tears, her joy. In that instant, it hit me: this was it. This was my lane. Weddings weren't just another line item on a schedule. They were memories in the making, and I was the one orchestrating them.

One of my earliest allies in that world was the head chef, Leclerc. He looked like Santa Claus; rosy cheeks, big belly and kind eyes; but he ran his kitchen with the discipline of a general. He'd sneak me hors d'oeuvres during tastings, teaching me how to describe flavors and textures to clients in a way that made them salivate. He became one of my biggest supporters, reminding me that clients didn't just want food; they wanted the feeling behind the food.

Hotel life wasn't without its lessons in betrayal. There was J, the banquet manager who was cunning, sly, and always angling for control. He was the kind of person who would smile to your face and then quietly set you up to fail. I learned that the hard way one afternoon when I needed to make a last-minute change to an event. In hotel terms, this was called a pop-up or a revision to a Banquet Event Order. A pop-up had to be stamped in red, reprinted, and redistributed to the entire team, with everyone knowing the new instructions had replaced the old. Because it was urgent, the turnaround time was often tight.

That day, I had a setup change that needed to be executed within forty-five minutes. Instead of wasting time running upstairs to write it out, stamping it, and then finding everyone to distribute it by hand, which was the standard process; I decided to just go straight to the source. I called J directly and gave him the change verbally, thinking it would be quicker. Rookie mistake. The change was never executed.

When the time came and we were confronted by the client as to why the change hadn't been done, J looked me dead in the eye with a blank stare and said we'd never spoken. He flat-out denied the entire conversation, leaving me standing there looking like I had dropped the ball.

At that moment, I knew I'd been played. Maybe he had forgotten and wanted to cover himself, or maybe he had set me up on purpose. Either way, it didn't matter. The result was the same and my credibility was on the line. That day was the first and last time I ever trusted anyone's word without proof when it came to my work. From then on, I lived by a rule that would carry me through my entire career: if it's not in writing, it never happened. Every conversation, every decision, every single change order was documented, by notes, email, or some other kind of paper trail. If a mistake was ever going to happen, I would own it. But I wasn't going to let anyone else's carelessness, or sabotage make me look like a fool again.

Then there was the Barton G event. That was the first time I witnessed an event go beyond linens and centerpieces and into full-blown theater. It featured Mermaid-tail chairs, florals cascading like underwater vines, and even servers in costume. It was a transformation so surreal that I thought: this is the future of events. I wasn't just inspired; I was electrified. I realized I didn't just want to plan events, I wanted to create timeless memories just like this.

The Radisson years toughened me up and polished me at the same time. I learned about hierarchy; how to respect it and also how to navigate around it when needed. I learned how to gain the trust of banquet staff, many of whom had been there for decades and didn't warm easily to newcomers. I learned how to balance client expectations with internal politics, and how to keep everyone, servers, chefs, managers, and brides moving toward the same goal. Within my first year at the Radisson, catering revenue nearly doubled. I wasn't just managing events; I was growing the business. Selling, upselling, and delivering at a level that made people trust me with more. That reputation followed me. When Chef Leclerc left the Radisson to join Fisher Island, he called me personally. He knew I was the girl who could "sell ice to an Eskimo." He knew I was his bingo card, the one who would guarantee results no matter where we worked.

It was here, in the heart of downtown Miami, that I stopped being "the girl with potential" and started being seen as a professional in her own right. The Radisson wasn't just a job; it was a proving ground. By the time I walked out of those doors, I had no doubt; event planning wasn't just something I was good at. It was what I was born to do.

A Planner in the Making

NEW YORK WEDDING, PHOTO CREDIT: JONATHAN SCOTT

Chapter 8

BUILT TO DAZZLE, TRAINED TO DELIVER

The call came from Chef Leclerc. By then, he had left the Radisson and taken a new position at Fisher Island. Having worked alongside me at the Radisson, he already knew my reputation as the girl who could "sell ice to an Eskimo," and there was only one phone call he was going to make. He wanted me to head the catering department and for him, it didn't matter that I was moving from a downtown hotel to one of the most luxurious private places in the world where the one percent vacationed or owned homes. What mattered was that I had the cultural background to parlay with Fisher Island's members; people from every corner of the globe, speaking in dollars and influence. My life had layered me for this moment; being Haitian, growing up in France, moving to the U.S., and even spending a semester studying abroad in Spain. On top of that, my family itself was a blend of cultures. My siblings had married across backgrounds so diverse; Orthodox Greek, Russian Jewish, German and Guadeloupean, that people used to joke and say we were like the United Nations. That kind of exposure put me at ease with people from all kinds of backgrounds. On Fisher Island, it all came together.

The first time I rode the ferry to the island, a single dolphin appeared in the water alongside the boat. For me, it was an omen, as if to say, this is where you belong. Yet when I walked into the banquet department, I realized this was going to be a different kind of proving ground. Fisher Island ran like its own universe, and the politics were as thick as the luxury was rich. Jose, the banquet manager, spearheaded the event staff; waiters, setup team, and bartenders. He had been there for decades, and nothing happened without his approval. The staff were loyal to him, not to outsiders like me. I had to earn my place, but that didn't take long. My numbers spoke for themselves. At the Radisson, catering revenue had almost doubled after I came on board, and Chef Leclerc knew that wasn't a coincidence. On Fisher Island, I brought that same drive, and soon Jose and I developed a rhythm. We became a duo. Clients would say "Guerdy and Jose" in one breath, as if we were a packaged deal. Together, we sold visions, not just menus. Sales doubled, then tripled. Commissions and gratuities flowed. These were the golden years.

The events themselves were on another level; a Make-A-Wish boat hop across the marina, a polo match that looked like something out of a movie, galas dripping in florals and chandeliers. I was moving in a world where members whispered about affairs, divorces, secret babies, and drugs over dinner at the Garwood Lounge. It was a playground for the rich. Discretion became currency. I learned fast that keeping my mouth shut was as valuable as any design I executed. One milestone was hosting my own baby shower on Fisher Island for my family and friends. It was for the birth of Miles, our firstborn son. The fact that I was able to afford to hold an event there was the real marker. It showed that all the hard work had paid off and that I had elevated myself into a different level of lifestyle. For a girl who once felt invisible, that celebration was the full-circle moment of belonging.

By the time I was deep into Fisher Island life, I had found a little escape that no one knew about. On my lunch breaks, I'd sneak over to a small flower shop owned by a woman named Martha. She was Cuban, in her 70s, with a thick accent and a very proper way about her. She had lived through the good years in Cuba before fleeing due to Castro, and she carried that nostalgia with her in the way she spoke and carried herself. At first, I went to the shop just to help, with her permission, of course. I didn't want anything to get lost in translation between her and the clients, so I'd step in to make sure orders came out right. What started as pitching in, grew into a friendship.

Then Martha got sick. It was cancer. Understandably, the shop became too much for her to run. Martha knew she wouldn't be able to sustain the business while seeking treatment. She decided that she would move to Arizona to live with her son and undergo care there, so the future of the shop was uncertain. That's when Russell and I sat down, and he suggested we take out an equity loan to buy the business. It was a huge decision, but we both knew opportunity when it knocked. The irony wasn't lost on me: I had never imagined being a florist. Planning was always the obvious path, yet here I was, a florist before a planner; and not just any florist, but one owning a shop in one of the most prestigious locations in the world.

By then, I had been working in catering on Fisher Island for three years. Running my own shop meant I had to resign. At least, that's what I thought. But when I handed in my resignation, they didn't want to let me go. Sales under my management had nearly tripled, and they knew no replacement could replicate the trust I had built with the demanding members. Instead, they agreed to keep me on, but on my own terms. I would subcontract as an independent, free to run the flower shop while also handling events. That arrangement is what truly launched the next phase of my career. No one else at the time had held both sides of the business as the florist and the planner. For clients, it was seamless: they could sit down with me once, give me all the details, and walk away knowing everything would be handled. I offered convenience, trust, and execution all bundled into one and it was more than just business.

Fisher Island was once owned by D. A. Dorsey, Miami's first Black millionaire, who allowed Black people to use his beach when they were barred from public ones. The irony, of course, is that the same island later became one of the wealthiest and most exclusive enclaves in the world. For me to become the first Black woman to own a business there was history coming full circle.

By the time I stepped fully into entrepreneurship, my reach had started to stretch far beyond Fisher Island. What began as one flower shop and one steady flow of island events quickly grew into something much larger. The demand outpaced the square footage, and before long I was running operations out of multiple warehouses. I started with two, then quickly expanded to four, as orders stacked up and events spilled outside of Fisher and into the wider Miami market. Each space was packed to the rafters with vases, candles, linens, and flowers arriving by the truckload.

But running a business tied to an island came with risks. If winds reached twenty-five miles per hour, the ferry would shut down. My staff, my inventory, even my clients could be stranded on one side or the other. Every weekend I held my breath, praying the weather didn't cancel access. Another challenge was the $5,200 monthly rent, the HOA fees, and the heavy taxes that came with operating on Fisher Island. I knew the setup wasn't sustainable forever. It was glamorous on the surface but brutal behind the scenes.

What made it all worthwhile was the trust that grew around my work. Fisher Island's demographic was predominantly Jewish families from New York, many splitting their time between the two cities. They celebrated their milestones under my chandeliers and trusted me to carry their traditions with care. That's when I started hearing the nickname "Rabbi Guerdy." It was said with affection, a recognition of how much faith they had in me to hold sacred moments without letting them break.

The bookings never stopped. This was before Instagram. People would hire through word of mouth, and in-network referrals carried my name from living rooms to boardrooms to beaches across South Florida. Other planners aspired to this level but rarely got access. I was in the center of it all, waving my wand like a fairy godmother. While J. Lo was playing a wedding planner on screen, I was the real-life wedding planner.

The clients reflected that rise. Diana Ross once performed at a wedding I worked on. Andrea Bocelli sang at a member's birthday party; his voice so powerful and captivating that the entire crowd froze in awe. I had the honor of planning Miami Heat star, Chris Bosh's wedding, and working closely with his father as part of the process. My weddings were known for their unforgettable after-parties; some featured performances from Wyclef Jean, Flo Rida, and more. These weren't just events; they were productions that cemented my place at the very top of the industry. But if there was one wedding that truly pushed me into another stratosphere, it was the wedding I did for Arielle Charnas, better known as Something Navy. She was one of the first fashion bloggers and influencers on Instagram, though at the time I wasn't even on the platform. Arielle encouraged me to join, explaining that it was the place to be seen. I trusted her instincts, and that decision changed everything.

In 2014, her wedding was hosted on Fisher Island, and I planned the entire event, handling both the design and logistics through my floral studio, Ocean Flowers. The guest list was a "who's who" of New York and *Brides Magazine* featured the event, which highlighted the lush green and white florals accented with a touch of plum. The ripple effect was immediate. The visibility of that wedding brought new eyes to my work and introduced me to an audience I never would have reached otherwise. Once I stepped onto the platform, the impact was undeniable. Soon after, I was hired to plan the wedding of Arielle's sister, Danielle, a top fashion stylist. Her wedding was later featured in Vogue. From there, the inquiries flooded in. That's the power of influence. People like to hire those who are trusted by the people they admire. Arielle's seal of approval cracked open doors I hadn't even knocked on yet.

It also broke me into legacy circles. The New York Jewish wedding community was known for its loyalty to vendors; the same planner or photographer often worked with families from childhood milestones all the way through adulthood. Brides were expected to use the family planner who had done their bat mitzvahs. But when those parents met me, I won them over instantly. They quickly realized I wasn't just another option; I was the right one. Once I delivered, they respected me for exceeding expectations. That was the moment I understood I wasn't just planning weddings anymore. I was shaping traditions, shifting expectations, and holding my own in spaces where legacy had always ruled. I had hated my name since I was little. Guerdy sounded harsh, sharp, and was constantly butchered. People often asked if it was short for Gertrude, which made it even worse. Depending on who was saying it, my name shifted into new sounds and syllables. In Spanish, it rolled out as Gweerdee, with a melodic rhythm that stretched into three beats. In French, it softened into Gairdee; delicate, with that faint Parisian "r" in the back of the throat. In Creole, it became Gehdee; quick and warm, like a smile you could hear. And in English, it often landed hard; Gurdee, flat, literal, and unmusical. I've heard every version, each one like a mirror reflecting where I was and who was speaking to me. Even though it was better than my original name, Elischéba, it still felt like a burden I was always having to explain, correct, and justify. But then something shifted. In the world of events, the name began to stand on its own. People would ask, "Who's doing the wedding? Oh, it's Guerdy?" and that was enough. My name became synonymous with excellence, uniqueness, and elevation. Guerdy wasn't just my name anymore; it was the signature. Guerdy meant GUERDYFY, and GUERDYFY meant the standard was elevated.

On the home front, life was shifting in big ways. In 2007, Russell and I welcomed our first son, Miles. Becoming parents changed the rhythm of everything, even as my business was climbing higher and higher. We had always planned to give Miles a sibling about two years later, but the reality was different. The demand for my work had reached a point where there was no pause button. I couldn't just step away. My name was on the line, and in this business, you're only as good as your last event.

Six years after Miles, in 2013, we finally welcomed Liam. His arrival completed our family in a way that was healing, though it never erased the memory of the daughter I didn't get to know, a loss whose story will find its place later in these pages.

For a while, things felt good. Business was booming, my family was healthy, and I was riding a wave I had worked so hard to catch. But life has a way of reminding you how fragile it all really is. Just when I thought I had found balance, the ground beneath me was about to shake to the core.

Built to Dazzle, Trained to Deliver

LA PALME MAGAZINE, PHOTO CREDIT: FILBERT KUNG

Chapter 9

MY BROTHER, EMMANUEL

At first, I was frozen in disbelief. I was in the kitchen making dinner when Russell called from work and asked me if I had seen the news. I immediately turned on the TV and it flashed across the screen. On January 12, 2010, at 4:53 p.m., a 7.0-magnitude earthquake struck Haiti just outside Port-au-Prince, and within seconds, the city fell to its knees. Concrete turned to dust, and the air filled with screams and ash. More than 220,000 people had lost their lives, while millions lost the roof over their heads. It wasn't just buildings that collapsed, it was history, hope, and the illusion of safety. For my family, it was the day the earth cracked and our hearts along with it.

Our family didn't always do a great job of attaching our past to our present. As we settled into new environments and focused on building our lives, I often thought about how meaningful it would be to go back to Haiti and connect on a deeper level. I wanted to see it not just as where we're from, but as a place still shaping who we are. Unfortunately, years of political instability have made it difficult for us to return safely, and with family now scattered across the world, we no longer had a stable foundation in Haiti to rebuild from. Still, that longing never goes away. The desire to return, to reconnect, to understand more, it was always there.

My brother Emmanuel, the eldest sibling, changed that for our family. Throughout the years, he carried the honor of being the family's storyteller, the one committed to stitching our history back together. He was tall and graceful, his features a clear reflection of our Taíno heritage. His decision to return to Haiti was about anchoring all of us to the motherland we came from and reconnecting the broken links between past and present while reminding us that identity isn't something you inherit once; it's something you tend to, over time. He wanted us to know Haiti not just through stories or family nostalgia, but through experience and presence. For him, going back wasn't just a homecoming; it was an act of restoration, a way of giving our family back its compass. Eventually, he and his wife, who both worked for the United Nations, made the big decision to settle in Haiti where they wanted to set a precedent for our entire family to finally begin the legacy reboot. It was his dream come true.

Emmanuel moved through the world with confidence and grace. That inner certainty became his power. My brother was magnetic. His presence filled every room, and not just with his looks. He was light, joyful and full of life. He loved tennis with a fiery passion. The Olympics were a sacred event in our home because Emmanuel would camp out in front of the T.V for every match. The French tennis star, Yannick Noah, was his idol. He even sported dreadlocks for a while, despite our religious parents being absolutely mortified by them as they said he looked like a vagabond. But, Emmanuel was unapologetically himself.

To our family, he was the trailblazer, the one who showed us what it looked like to turn dreams into reality. In France, he stood out early on, earning a spot in an exchange program to England, which meant he came to the U.S. already comfortable with the language the rest of us were still learning. He was also the only one who actually understood the lyrics to "Billie Jean" and all those other American hits we used to mumble our way through. Later, he became the first in our family to go to college, earning a scholarship to the University of Miami, a milestone that made us all proud. He was the one who, everywhere he went, both in France and in Miami, was considered the cool kid from the very beginning. He had a natural and effortless energy about him and was the heartbeat of the family. His achievements raised the bar for the rest of us. His work with the United Nations took him to the frontlines of conflict in Kosovo, Rwanda, and other war zones across Africa. He thrived in his work, building peace in places falling apart. Ironically, the only place he wouldn't be safe was the one that gave him life: Haiti.

It's never easy for me to revisit these memories as they sit in a place I don't touch often. But to the best of my recollection, here's what I remember.

The day the earthquake hit, my brother was at home with his three girls. They had just finished tennis practice and were settling in for the evening. The two oldest were getting ready for dinner and bedtime, while the youngest was still by his side. That small detail is what saved her life. When the ground began to shake, he instinctively covered her with his body, shielding her completely.

She was the only survivor, found beneath him with a broken leg but a steady heartbeat. Rescuers pulled her from the rubble and she was taken to the Dominican Republic for medical care, along with her mother, who was now a widow. They were later brought to my home in Miami, where we began to piece together what had happened.

As for my two other nieces, those angels went to heaven escorted by their brave father, my dear brother.

The days we waited for their three bodies to be recovered were grueling. There was almost no organized rescue effort at the time. Everyone was digging for their own loved ones. My brother's wife was able to get help faster than most because she had access to a satellite phone, but even then, it took time—long, unbearable time—to bring them home.

During that waiting period, since Miami was one of the closest points of access to Haiti, my home became the base for both families. My relatives and hers who flew in from New Zealand, all stayed with us. The house was full, yet it felt unbearably quiet. The air was heavy with the kind of silence that hums with pain. Those minutes, hours, and months were brutal. We tried to keep the children shielded from it; Miles was two and a half at the time, and my niece, who was only a few months younger, needed love, safety, and laughter. They played together on the floor or took rides in Miles' wagon while we waited for the phone to ring with news. We cried in shifts, mourning privately in corners, and whispering prayers while pretending everything was okay in front of them.

What I remember most about that time was the tea. My sister-in-law's family, being from New Zealand and shaped by their English heritage, loved their tea. The kettle was on all day long, filling the house with a sound that somehow made things feel a little more bearable. No matter what was happening, someone was always boiling water, pouring cups and passing mugs around. It became its own ritual; a quiet kind of comfort that filled the silence we couldn't bear. Even now, the whistle of the kettle, that simple, familiar sound still reminds me of those days.

After an event like that, you can never be whole again, no matter what. It wasn't fair. It was too sudden. It wasn't right. Yet somehow, we had to find the strength to keep going; not for ourselves, but for his surviving daughter.

She lives with her mother, and is now pursuing a career in music. She is radiant, slim, athletic, musical, and brilliant. When I see her, I see him. I feel him. Through her, he lives. She doesn't want pity. Like all of us, she is a survivor. She carries an old soul, not by choice but by necessity.

Emmanuel would be so proud. He is proud. I know it. His story didn't end in that rubble; it lives on in his daughter, in the soil of Haiti, and in all of us who still remember. For that reason, I will never stop telling his story. His legacy will live on.

My brother and I were both Capricorns, but we carried it differently. I'm a January Capricorn; structured, organized, and always planning the next move. Emmanuel was a December Capricorn; born on Christmas Day, and that alone says a lot. He had a lightness about him, an ease that drew people in.

Where I was focused and driven, he was calm and magnetic. He made things look effortless. Being a Christmas baby suited him, he just had this way of making people feel seen, like his presence itself was a gift. We had the kind of relationship that picked up like no time had passed. When he came to Miami, he'd stay with Russell and I, and we'd laugh, eat, and catch up like no months, years, or miles had ever come between us. He had that rare gift of lightness. He never let sorrow settle in. He lived by a code of joy and he always held a deep connection to Haiti. Being the oldest, he remembered the most. He dreamed of returning, investing, and rebuilding. When he got married, he chose Labadie, which sits on a stretch of Haitian coastline that cruise lines market as a private island stop "near Haiti." But it isn't near Haiti; it is Haiti.

Emmanuel wanted to honor that truth and to celebrate Haiti for what it really is: a hidden paradise. I was super excited to be going back to my birth country for the wedding and in the days leading up to my flight, everything in Haiti had been calm. My family members, who were traveling from different parts of the world had already made it to Labadie without any issues. They described their trips as smooth, sentimental, and even nostalgic. For many of them, it was their first time back and just setting foot on Haitian soil brought back waves of emotion. It all sounded beautiful, exactly the kind of homecoming I had been dreaming of, since I was too young to remember my homeland and I was eager to finally feel that connection for myself.

But on the morning of my flight, everything changed. Haiti was beginning to see early signs of political unrest as small gatherings were forming both for, and against, then Haitian, President Jean-Bertrand Aristide. It was still a developing story at the time, not yet the full-scale chaos it would later become. The airport remained open and flights were still departing. I told myself it would be fine. That morning's flight was meant to take me to Haiti in time for my brother's welcome dinner the night before his wedding ceremony, but instead, it became the day the country erupted. Add to that a gloomy weather forecast, and it felt like every possible obstacle was lining up to keep me from getting to Labadie for his special day.

One of my older sisters, who at the time also lived in Miami, had planned to travel with me. Once on the plane, our flight was nearly canceled because of the storms and the violent protests that were beginning to spread across the capital in Port-au-Prince. The captain made an announcement explaining that the situation was being monitored closely and gave anyone who felt unsafe the option to deboard. My sister had an anxiety attack and backed out at the last minute, terrified. Meanwhile, Russell, who had dropped us off at the airport and was already back at home, had just learned that the brewing unrest was indeed escalating and became frightened for us.

He called me while I was still on the plane, just before takeoff, and demanded I come home. He had never spoken to me like that before, with fear wrapped in authority. But I couldn't turn back. I had to go, so I went alone, a Capricorn through and through; stubborn and determined.

From Miami, I first landed in Port-au-Prince before connecting to a small local flight headed to Cap-Haïtien. That second flight was in one of those tiny planes with only a few rows of seats where you can see straight into the cockpit, and it was rough. As we took off, the sky darkened, and within minutes, rain was hitting the windows hard, almost sideways. I could hear the metal creak as we climbed through the storm. The turbulence was relentless; it felt like the plane was being tossed around like a toy. My stomach lifted and dropped with every sudden dip, and I gripped the armrest, trying to steady my breathing.

In my head, I started having a quiet conversation with myself; should anything happen to me during this journey.... I prayed, asking God for forgiveness for defying Russell's warning not to go, and prayed that he could find it in his heart to forgive me if I didn't make it back. The storm wasn't a drizzle, it felt like a hurricane. While the plane was shaking hard and fighting to stay level, all I could do was sit still and keep praying.

When we finally started descending toward Cap-Haïtien, I felt every muscle in my body unclench. While I was just grateful to be back on solid ground, that relief didn't last long. The drive from the airport to the ferry made it clear that the situation in the country had worsened since I'd taken off from Miami. The unpaved road added to the instability as the car jerked and bounced as we made our way through crowds of people shouting and waving flags. Burning tires sent thick smoke across the street, and at times, bystanders banged on the car as we tried to inch forward. My brother had sent a security guard along with the driver to meet me, but even with that, it was terrifying. Anything could have happened at any moment, but thankfully I made it to the harbor.

The last leg of the journey was the ferry ride to Labadie. The trip from Cap-Haïtien to Labadie is only about six or seven miles, a short crossing that usually takes twenty minutes at most. But, that night, the storm made it feel endless. The sea was restless, slamming against the sides of the boat as we lurched forward in the dark. Rain blurred the horizon and every crash of water felt like a warning, but I held on, soaked, shivering, and whispering prayers under my breath. What should have been a quick trip stretched into nearly forty-five minutes of blind faith. As the boat drew closer to Labadie, I could make out the familiar silhouettes of my family through the rain. They were inside a large, beautiful stone house, eating, laughing and completely unaware that I was almost there. Then I noticed a few children on the beach, waving and shouting toward the house as they saw me. Within seconds, everyone came running outside. When I finally stepped onto the shore, we all stood there in the rain, hugging, crying, and grateful that I had made it. They had been worried sick, as no one had been able to reach me because I had no cellular signal during my journey. Everyone who could make it there had been waiting and holding their breath for any sign of me. I was finally able to call Russell who had a mix of anger and relief in his voice, but within seconds, I could tell he was too happy that I was alive to stay mad. He knew what I had risked to be there, and I knew it was worth everything.

    The next 24 hours, I felt something I hadn't felt in a long time: belonging. That night was magical. We drank, we laughed, and we danced barefoot in the sand. The wedding the next morning was simple yet sacred. Palm leaves and hibiscus bloom formed the altar and there they stood taking their wedding vows witnessed by the handful of us. My brother's wedding was the most memorable one I've ever experienced, even including my own, because of where it happened and what it represented. I could have married Russell anywhere and felt the same love I do now as our bond isn't defined by a place. But my brother's wedding was different. It was about the land itself; the same soil we were born on and the same air our ancestors breathed. Standing there felt bigger than a celebration; it felt sacred, like love and legacy had finally met on the same ground.

EMMANUEL WITH HIS TWO GIRLS, KOFIE-JADE & ZENZIE

GUERDY & EMMANUEL AT HIS WEDDING IN LABADIE, HAITI

Chapter 10

TAP TAP TAP

I never thought I would see the day when the same place that once gave me paradise would later become the setting for such great loss. It's strange how one place can hold both one of the best and one of the worst days of your life. For me, Haiti became that place; the soil of celebration and devastation, joy and heartbreak, all in one. Right before Emmanuel moved to live and work in Haiti, he came to visit me in Miami along with his wife and their three beautiful daughters in tow.

During his visit, I took him to Fisher Island to see the island and my floral studio. He was impressed, so much so that he asked to invest in my business. I declined. I'd always heard not to mix family and business, and I loved our bond too much to risk it. But after he was gone, that choice echoed louder than I ever expected. It became the space where my grief settled.

They say grief comes in stages; denial to soften the blow, anger to release it, bargaining to make sense of it, depression to sit with it, and acceptance to move beyond it. But no one tells you those stages don't come in order, or that sometimes you loop through them like a song stuck on repeat. For me, bargaining was the verse I couldn't stop replaying. It was the space where I kept trying to make sense of loss, as if logic could soften something that wasn't meant to make sense at all.

After weeks of crying every day, the kind of tears that come in waves and leave you hollow, the tears finally slowed. But they never truly stopped. They just changed shape, turning into long hours, endless work, and a mission that bordered on obsession. Emmanuel had believed in me, so much so that he wanted to invest in my business before he died. After losing him, that decision haunted me. I couldn't go back and say yes, so I tried to make that "no" count for something. That became my unspoken pact with him: to work harder, aim higher, and achieve more, as if success could somehow bridge the distance between us. I wasn't chasing validation anymore; I was chasing redemption. Each milestone became a silent conversation with my brother. Each achievement, a whisper, "Do you see me now?"

It wasn't about ambition anymore, it was grief turned into motion. As if by moving faster, I could outrun the pain. But grief doesn't let you get far. It moves with you, quietly pushing the finish line just a little further every time you think you've reached it. I missed him; his voice, his humor, the way he made ordinary moments feel like stories worth telling. I missed my nieces; their laughter, their energy, the life they carried that was snatched away too soon. That kind of loss doesn't just hurt; it hollows you out.

So instead, I became something. I turned myself into an investment. My success would have to be his dividend. My rise, his return. I remember whispering to myself, "I'll make you all proud, you'll see." And I meant it. It went from ambition to obsession. I GUERDYFY'd everything in sight. I was already doing extremely well, not only producing weddings up and down the Florida coast but also in New York and the Hamptons, where many of my Fisher Island clients lived and flew me up for their celebrations. But after Emmanuel's death, I pushed harder. I started taking on more events, flying internationally with increasing frequency; Mexico, the Bahamas, Jamaica, Turks and Caicos, Portugal, and so on; because when grief knocks the wind out of you, motion feels like oxygen. I was building at a pace no one could match, not because I wanted to beat the competition, but because I didn't want to disappoint my brother. There was no Plan B. Just Plan Prove Him Right. Then the bird came. A few months after his passing, I noticed a small bird tapping at my home office window; the same spot and same rhythm, day after day. Tap. Tap. Tap. It felt like a visitation. I took it as a sign that Emmanuel was checking in, cheering me on, and whispering, "You've got this. Keep going. Keep building". And so I did. At the time, I didn't even question it. The idea that he was there, urging me forward, gave me comfort. Every tap felt like confirmation. Yes, keep going; yes, make it count; yes, don't stop now. I convinced myself he was my invisible coach, still guiding me, still invested, still counting on me to turn loss into legacy.

Over time, something began to shift. The rhythm of the tapping started to feel different, less like applause, more like interruption. What if I'd misunderstood the message? What if the bird wasn't telling me to go harder, but pleading with me to slow down? What if it wasn't encouragement, but a warning, like a tiny hand tapping from the other side of the glass saying, "Enough. You've done enough".

That thought haunted me. Deep down, I knew I had been running on fumes, using productivity as protection. I told myself I was honoring him, but maybe I was just avoiding stillness. Maybe, the bird had been trying to reach through that blur of motion to remind me that grief doesn't always want you to move, it sometimes just wants you to feel. Maybe it was Emmanuel, begging me to pause, to heal, to listen. Maybe the tapping was him saying, "You don't have to earn my pride, it's already yours." But, I wasn't ready to hear anything except the roar of my own to-do list. Slowing down would have meant facing what I had buried beneath the busy. And so I didn't.

**GUERDY WITH HER FLORAL/PRODUCTION TEAM
AT EVENT SITE SETTING UP**

Tap Tap Tap

GUERDY READY FOR A WEDDING CEREMONY, MIAMI

Chapter 11

THE "NO" THAT MADE ME DANGEROUS

Grief had made me productive and filled the silence with noise, but it didn't quiet the ache. I mistook motion for healing. I kept pushing forward because stopping meant sitting in the stillness, and that was unbearable. Work became my medicine, my distraction, and my armor. If I just stayed busy enough, maybe I could outpace the pain. Then came a wedding that carried the same defiance pulsing through me; a test, a mirror, a moment that would show exactly how far I was willing to go. I received a call from a mother of a bride asking if I'd consider planning her daughter's wedding at a well-known private venue. I said yes, until I realized that the venue itself had other plans. This venue had a history that wasn't spoken about publicly but lived in its walls. Decades ago, it was the kind of establishment that proudly displayed the words "no Jews, no Blacks."

They no longer used those exact words, of course, but that same undertone still lingered. You could feel it in the air the minute you walked through the doors. It carried that "inner circle" air. Decades ago, that kind of circle was made up of men, but over time it evolved into something less about gender and more about gatekeeping. The people within it were talented, but the system itself was self-serving. It catered to what was best for the institution, not for the client. That's what kept the monotony alive: the same vendors, the same look, the same energy, all recycled under the comforting illusion of tradition.

The venue operated on what they called a "preferred vendor list," which was meant to sound professional but was just a gatekeeping system in disguise. It featured the same vendors who had dominated the scene twenty years earlier; the planners, florists, and photographers; protected by name recognition and old relationships. Meanwhile, a whole generation of new talent was being overlooked. Planners with cutting-edge ideas and modern sensibilities couldn't even get a foot in the door.

And that's what made it sting, I wasn't some unknown beginner. I had already proved myself. I owned a floral studio on Fisher Island, one of the most exclusive private clubs in the country. I had executed luxury events for clients who expected, and received perfection. Yet, despite all that, I was being denied access to this space, and it wasn't because of my work or reputation. I later found out that this wasn't a one-time thing. My name had been coming up for years during client inquiries, and every time, the conversation was cut short. The venue would redirect the couple to one of their "approved" planners before I ever had a chance to pitch. They didn't just close the door, they locked it before I could even knock. In some cases, the recommended planners weren't even based in Florida and had never executed a major event at that property, yet somehow, they stayed on the list.

When I finally received my first inquiry to plan a wedding at that venue, the client, a mother-of-the-bride, admitted she'd been confused. She'd asked about me and was told I wasn't on their preferred vendor list, which didn't make sense to her. She knew my work, her friends had hosted events with me on Fisher Island and at venues across the country. She couldn't understand why I wasn't allowed through the same doors. She told me about meeting the "approved" planner and being shocked when that planner arrived late, hair tied back in a bun, wearing yoga pants and had no sense of urgency, as if her position on that list guaranteed her the job. The client left that meeting furious and embarrassed for even entertaining it. When she complained, the venue brushed her off, making excuses that it was the holidays and that the planner was traveling.

Instead of waiting for a second meeting with their planner, the client reached out to me directly to arrange a meeting with me instead. I arrived on time with my heels clicking with intention as I entered the room. My iPad was charged and my vision board presentation ready. By the end of our meeting, the client was sold. That's when I decided to challenge her. I told her plainly, "If you really want to work with me, then make them explain why you can't." I encouraged her to remind them that this was her wedding, not theirs. God bless her, right then and there, she called the venue's director in front of me and said, "If Guerdy doesn't do my wedding, I'm taking my daughter's wedding elsewhere." That single sentence cracked their foundation. Suddenly, they were forced to reconsider. They made it clear that this would be a one-time exception as if allowing me in was some kind of stretch for them. It didn't bother me. Because I knew that once the door was open, even a crack, I'd find a way to kick it wide open, and that's exactly what happened. I executed that wedding flawlessly; every detail, every transition, and every design element was seamless. The word spread fast, because in this industry, three hundred impressed wedding guests turns into three hundred walking testimonials overnight. What the venue thought would be a one-time exception became the moment they realized they couldn't put the genie back in the bottle. But I didn't stop with my own win. I always matched my clients with the best vendors for their vision, regardless of venue politics. For that first wedding, I recommended an Asian-owned floral company known for sourcing the largest, most unique Phalaenopsis orchids from around the world. The client wanted that specific look, and they were the only team that could achieve it. I owned my own floral company, but I put my ego aside. It wasn't about me, it was about matching the client with the perfect partner. I refused to become what the venue had been to me. I had to be the example. Their artistry was unmatched, but they weren't on the list either. I fought for them just like I had fought for myself. The venue finally agreed, once again claiming, "one-time exception."

The wedding went beautifully, and within months, that same floral company was hired twice more at that same property. The door was now open. Next, I pushed for a Jewish-owned floral company because of their signature style that perfectly matched the client's vision. Same resistance. Same excuses. Same outcome. They executed beautifully, and once again, the venue had to swallow its pride. This was no longer coincidence, it was change. Every time I walked through that door, I held it open behind me, that's what made me dangerous: my tenacity. Breaking through that venue's ceiling meant more than professional success. Every "no" I challenged was really me answering the one I never got to change. It was about rewriting the script, about proving that "no" is never final. Over the next twelve years, I stayed in that state of motion: high-functioning depression, as my friend, Dr. Judith Joseph, would call it.

But I also learned that sometimes I had to be the one to say no, especially when integrity was on the line. So, here's the full story of that wedding where the groom said "no" at the altar. Everything seemed set in place as far as planning and logistics were concerned, until the morning of the wedding, when the bride copied me on an email to friends canceling the ceremony. In panic, I tried contacting her to see if this was some kind of mistake. A few hours later, she sent another email saying the wedding was back on. As a planner, that's never a good sign; something was definitely off. It's one thing to manage last-minute nerves, but this felt different. These were two indecisive people in their mid-fifties about to make one of the most permanent commitments of their lives, and I had to steady the ship long enough to get them to the aisle. After that cancellation scare, it was smooth sailing, until the ceremony.

The ceremony took place under a grand banyan tree with a beautiful altar draped in fabric and flowers, the kind of setup that looked like it belonged in a movie. Champagne was passed around as guests arrived before seating began. You could tell they were anxious to witness this telenovela unfold, especially after receiving the false-alarm email earlier that day. Both the bride and groom were walked down the aisle by their children, all in their teens, standing there with that mix of pride and unease that only comes from watching your parents remarry. When it came time to exchange vows, everyone leaned in with anticipation, waiting for that emotional "I do" moment that seals the deal. But instead, when it was the groom's turn to speak, he looked at her, paused, and said quietly but clearly, "I love you, but I just can't do this."

The air seemed to crack in half. Gasps rippled through the guests as the groom turned and walked away, his three children following close behind. For a moment, no one moved. The bride's sister broke the silence, shouting, "You snake!" while the bride just stood there, hands on her hips, staring him down in disbelief. It was the kind of moment that doesn't fade with time; you could feel the shock carve itself into the air.

I took a slow breath, scanning the scene, my planner instincts kicking in even as my heart dropped. My job had always been to manage chaos, but this was something else entirely: a wedding unraveling in real time. Guests were frozen, unsure whether to sit, leave, or comfort the bride. Then came the hardest part: deciding what to do next. I went to check on the bride first, who was lingering among guests, visibly shaken but trying to stay composed as friends surrounded her in comfort. Then I approached the groom.

Technically, he was the one who had paid for the wedding, and I needed to know what he intended to do. I assumed he'd be the one to leave, given he had already walked away from the altar without shame. However, he looked at me calmly and said that since he had paid for it all, he planned to stay and asked that I ensure the bride was off the premises so he could continue the evening; as if to say, I paid for it, so I'll get my money's worth.

Internally, I was stunned, but outwardly, I remained composed. I quietly instructed my catering team to proceed with the food and beverage services as those obligations fell under their contract. But, as I stood there processing it all, I realized that my own agreement was tied to performing a wedding service, and no wedding had taken place. Continuing to operate as if it had taken place felt tone-deaf to the reality unfolding around us. A bride had just been humiliated in front of her children, and I couldn't pretend it was business as usual. My responsibility, my boundaries, and my integrity were all on the line.

My planning services had been fulfilled, and while the catering would continue as contracted, I made the decision that my part was officially done. I went back to my office to write up a formal report of the night's events, documenting every detail for my records. Later that evening, when I returned to the ballroom to check on things one last time, I saw the groom being lifted up on a chair like it was a bar mitzvah, and that was my cue to exit stage left. My role was finished, and my conscience was clear.

I quietly gathered my belongings and walked out, knowing I had done the right thing. Months later, I read that the couple had reconciled and gotten married, which I couldn't believe; but if they liked it, I loved it. Years later, however, I also heard they had divorced. What a roller coaster. That night taught me that saying no isn't always about defiance, it's about dignity, and sometimes the most powerful "no" is the one you say to protect your values. When COVID-19 hit in 2020, it threatened the rhythm of my grind and, for the first time in years, forced the world, and me to stop. Everything shut down. Events were canceled or postponed indefinitely. At first, it felt strange not to have back-to-back deadlines or flight itineraries waiting. But for a while, I loved it. I got to slow down and really be with Russell and the boys in a way that felt grounding. We found our rhythm. Russell, as a first responder, would come home every day like a Transformer, shedding his gear at the door before stepping inside. We cooked together, laughed together, and found comfort in the rare gift of stillness. But even in that calm, a part of me was still restless, itching to create again and build something new.

While catching up with an industry friend and brainstorming business ideas that might work during such a strange time, he suggested starting a company that provided on-site COVID testing for weddings and events. There were a few of us involved as investors, and I agreed immediately. Within weeks, we had corporate and private clients. I was a silent investor. As the first phase of COVID restrictions loosened and micro-weddings became permissible again, I was one of the first planners back at it, producing small, perfectly measured celebrations that followed every rule of social distancing, masks, and testing. Precision became the new luxury. I was fortunate to have clients with the resources and space to host private events in their lush backyards that looked like full-scale venues.

When larger functions were finally allowed again, many venues struggled to refill their calendars. Ironically, one of the first large-scale weddings I produced after restrictions lifted took place at the very same venue that had once refused to let me in. By that time, I had done over ten weddings there. This particular one was a full buyout as the client purchased every ballroom and adjacent space to keep guests separate from the public. The world had been shaken to its core, and for the couple, this wedding was a celebration of survival, resilience, and gratitude; they went all out. An A-list artist was flown in from New York to perform at their wedding for a private thirty-minute piano set; the piano delivered from her own studio, custom-tuned on site, and positioned under a spotlight that made the room go silent the moment she played.

While the industry was still finding its footing, the world was forced to face something deeper. When the world watched George Floyd take his last breath under a police officer's knee, the country was forced to confront what many of us already knew: that injustice isn't always loud. Sometimes it's woven quietly into systems that pretend to be fair. As a mother of two black boys, it landed in my chest. We've raised our kids to work hard and to earn success by merit, but we also taught them awareness, because pretending the world is fair doesn't make it so. They have to understand that excellence might still be questioned, that rooms might still try to gatekeep them, and that none of that means they don't belong, it means they must walk in prepared.

That national reckoning made me think of my own quiet protests; the moments I had refused to take "no" as a verdict, and the battles I had fought to be seen and allowed in; to stay in. It reminded me that every door I had pushed through wasn't just for me; it was for everyone watching from the outside, wondering if they could, too. It also made me think about how merit was the throughline all along. DEI wasn't about handing out spots, it was about expanding the table for those who had already earned their place but were locked out. The irony was, my story with that venue had been a kind of reverse DEI; they had been "profiling" for legacy, not progress. But I had proved that merit had always been the true qualifier. Yet sometimes I think back on what I thought was breaking barriers and wonder if, in trying to prove I belonged everywhere, I stopped asking whether I even wanted to be everywhere.

Looking back, I realize that sometimes survival disguises itself as drive, and the very thing that saves you for a season can break you if you never pause to breathe. I didn't know it yet, but that lesson was waiting for me, louder, harder, and completely unignorable.

The "NO" That Made Me Dangerous

GUERDY IN PLANNING MODE

Chapter 12

SCHEDULED FOR COLLAPSE

My work spoke for itself, but so did my body. The long hours, the sleepless nights, the constant motion all began to show. I had been through a lot physically and emotionally, and though my career was at its peak, I was running on empty.

When I got pregnant again after Miles, it had been about five years. Five years of building, hustling, and believing that everything was under control. I was about fourteen weeks along when we finally shared the news with our family; Miles, my parents, his parents, and my siblings. For the first time in a long time, I felt still, and even content. I thought it would be smooth sailing, just as carrying Miles had been.

But things were about to take a turn for the worse. One of my sisters was visiting at the time, and one evening we decided to take a walk with our Rhodesian Ridgeback, Rocco. He was strong and full of energy, the kind of dog who always wanted to lead and loved his walks. As we stepped out of the front door, he suddenly lunged forward after spotting a squirrel, jerking the leash so hard that it caught me off guard. My foot missed the step, and I stumbled down hard. It was an awkward, jarring drop that sent a shock through my whole body. For a second, I froze, trying to convince myself it was nothing. But something in the way I landed told me otherwise. It didn't look catastrophic, but deep down I knew something had gone wrong. It was that quiet, instinctive knowing, your body whispers before your mind catches up. I didn't brush it off, I called my gynecologist immediately and rushed to the first available appointment I could get, desperate for reassurance.

During the ultrasound, my worst fear was confirmed, there was no heartbeat. The silence in that room was deafening. I remember staring at the monitor, hoping the machine was wrong. It wasn't. My doctor gently explained that I'd need a D&C procedure to remove the fetal tissue. Even though, deep down, I'd sensed it was coming, hearing those words felt like the ground had been pulled from beneath me. I walked out numb, carrying a quiet grief that only mothers who've lost can truly understand.

Later, when the results came back and we learned that the baby was a girl, it pierced deeper. I was surprised, it had never crossed my mind that I would have a daughter. I had always pictured myself as a boy mom; maybe because I grew up surrounded by brothers or maybe because life had trained me to stay strong. But knowing she was a girl shifted something in me. Losing her felt like losing a softer side of myself I hadn't yet met. To cope, I told myself that maybe God had made a mistake and took her back so He could give me what was meant for me all along, another son. It was the only way I could survive that kind of pain. Deep down, though, I sometimes wondered if I wasn't meant to have a girl because I feared she would go through the same things I did. Maybe the reflection of that pain would have been too much to bear. And with the way my work consumed me, the guilt of not being fully present for a daughter would have broken me twice over.

When we were clear to try again, we got pregnant immediately, and soon after, Liam arrived. He was my rainbow after the storm, proof that love and life could still find their way through loss. But having him also came with its own physical and emotional toll. I had a C-section, and the recovery was brutal, and unlike anything I'd experienced before. I spent weeks sitting still and healing. While doing so, I watched the weight stay on, unable to move the way I once could.

I gained nearly sixty pounds and still had forty left to lose when the fog of newborn life began to lift. As much as I was enjoying my new bundle of joy, I also wanted to feel like myself again. I yearned to feel confident, feminine, and strong once again. I wanted to reconnect with the woman I'd been before, physically. So, as a start, I decided to get teardrop implants placed behind the muscle of my breast to enhance my shape and bring back the balance I'd lost after pregnancy. I also had some liposuction around my midsection to refine my silhouette. I never wanted anything flashy, I just wanted to put the pieces back together. In fact, no one even noticed I'd had implants; they looked completely natural. When I looked in the mirror afterward, I finally recognized the woman staring back. I felt good again, not perfect, but whole. But the truth is, I still had about forty pounds left to lose, even after all those quick fixes.

One day, I met a friend for lunch at a restaurant. I got there early, looked around, and didn't see her anywhere. Then I heard, "Guerdy, don't you see me? I'm right here!" I turned and almost didn't recognize her. She looked incredible; slim, radiant, and full of energy. When I asked what she'd done, she mentioned a dietitian who had helped her manage her appetite and metabolism. That same week, I made an appointment. After running full bloodwork to make sure everything was aligned, he recommended an appetite-suppressant supplement designed to help me sustain my intermittent-fasting routine. My workdays were long and unpredictable, and it helped me manage hunger while keeping up with my schedule, especially during marathon event days. But over time, what started as convenience became routine. Meals disappeared, and exhaustion became normal. I wasn't listening to my body anymore, I was managing it like another project.

That routine slowly became my new normal. I didn't see it as a problem, I saw it as proof of my discipline. Initially, since we trusted each other's independence, Russell didn't question it much. But over time, he started to notice the changes. He saw how thin I'd gotten and how the circles under my eyes deepened. The toll of it all, the constant travel, the sleepless nights, the nonstop workload, and the dieting was starting to show. He was telling me to find balance and to remember my health. It was taking a toll, and this time his voice hit differently. When he said it, I listened. For the first time, I started to pull back. I started saying no to certain events and cutting down on travel. I started realizing that I couldn't keep going at that pace without something breaking.

Slowing down felt uncomfortable at first. For someone like me, motion had always meant progress, but even as I took small steps to pull back, I still thought I was in control. I had no idea what was already unfolding beneath the surface. I'd already lived a version of this before; the moment when life is moving beautifully forward, and then, without warning, it's taken from you. Losing that pregnancy taught me how fragile even the strongest body can be. I just didn't realize that my own body was once again preparing to stop me in my tracks, not through loss of a child this time, but through a reckoning that would demand everything of me. The same body that once created life was now warning me to save my own. The collapse wasn't coming. It had already been scheduled.

**GUERDY AT A WEDDING VENUE, PHOTO CREDIT:
ADAGION PHOTOGRAPHY**

PART II

THE JOURNEY TO "ME"

PHOTO CREDIT: JIM JORDAN PHOTOGRAPHY

Chapter 13

PARADISE, INTERRUPTED

L ife had finally started to slow down a bit before that trip. After years of saying yes to everything and everyone, I had started to listen to Russell's warning that I was working too hard. He'd been telling me for months that I needed to slow down, to protect my peace, and to give my body a chance to breathe. For once, I listened. I began taking projects more selectively; only from past clients, referrals, and people I genuinely trusted. It was my way of finding balance without feeling like I was losing momentum. I thought I had finally found that sweet spot where I could still create and still deliver, but at a pace that didn't feel like it was costing me my health. I didn't know it yet, but that shift in pace was what made what came next hit even harder.

Paradise, Interrupted

It was March of 2023 when I boarded the plane for Saint Barts; one of those places that made you instantly exhale. Everything about it felt calm but elevated: the ocean, the people, the food, the vibe. My friend Jenni was married there ten years earlier at Eden Rock, one of the most well-known hotels on the island. That wedding had been a dream, and now she wanted to celebrate her upcoming ten-year anniversary, marking the milestone with another unforgettable weekend in the same place where it all began. So, on this planning trip, I was there not just as her best friend, but as her planner and the one responsible for bringing the magic back full circle. This was a pre-anniversary visit to scout locations and gather logistics to map out every single detail to GUERDYFY her celebration. She was renting the Rockstar Villa for the big celebration weekend, which was easily the most famous and coveted suite on the island. The villa was massive; over 16,000 square feet of pure indulgence, with four master suites, a private recording studio, a screening room, and its own gate that opened directly onto the Beach. Inside, everything felt curated down to the last detail; black-and-white marble floors, sleek modern furniture, walls of glass overlooking the ocean, and even a bar and dining room designed by the famous French industrial designer, Philippe Starck. Outside, an infinity pool sat on a raised terrace that overlooked the beach where the vow renewal ceremony would take place; a view so breathtaking it almost felt like part of the design plan. It wasn't just a villa, it was an experience, the kind of place where luxury didn't shout, it whispered. At roughly twenty thousand dollars a night, the villa would be where Jenni and her immediate family would stay for the week, while the actual reception itself would take place at the Eden Rock restaurant for a rare, full buyout for the night. We also had a few other venues lined up for the weekend; for the welcome reception the night before, a farewell brunch, and other events like the after-party and smaller gatherings throughout.

It felt like such a full-circle moment for her, and I was honored to be the one helping her make it happen. There were five of us on this girls trip: Jenni, myself and three other friends. Since Jenni hated flying on small planes, we landed on a neighboring island first, then took a private charter yacht across to Saint Barts. By the time we arrived, our hair was windswept and we were all smiles. That first night, we stayed at Cheval Blanc, which was absolutely beautiful. We had dinner at L'Isola, a local Italian spot everyone loves, and the next day we started beach club hopping to finalize the venues for her welcome dinner and Sunday brunch. We visited La Guérite, La Toiny and Nikki Beach, taking in each of their special beach club vibes. The energy was easy and genuine, no pretentiousness, no influencer behavior, just five women enjoying life, laughing, and switching between glam mode and casual mode without missing a beat. Jenni and I had range. We both came from humble beginnings, and even though we could blend into a room full of billionaires, we were just as comfortable cracking jokes in bikinis and flip-flops.

The first two days were perfect. The weather, the company, the flow of the trip, it all felt aligned. But on the third morning, everything changed. My phone rang while I was getting ready, and I saw that it was my gynecologist. I had recently gone for my annual mammogram. I'd started them early, before turning forty because when I went in for my breast implant surgery, they found a lot of density and calcification in my breasts. As a precaution, they sent me for a mammogram before clearing me for the procedure. From that point on, regular monitoring became part of my life. It had become routine, something I didn't even think twice about anymore. All of a sudden, I realized that the testing this time around had not been routine. I had been asked back to do a follow up mammogram, and then undergone a biopsy several days before the trip. So, when I saw the call that morning, I froze. Something in me just knew. I answered, and he said, "Hello, Guerdy, your test results came back." I stopped him before he could continue. "Hold on," I said. "Let me merge Russell into the call." I didn't want to hear whatever was coming next alone. Deep down, I already knew it wasn't good.

I stood there in paradise on the phone, Russell silent on the other end, and the doctor's voice suddenly making everything around me fade. "It's DCIS," he said. "Stage 0." Ductal Carcinoma In Situ. Non-invasive. It was early. Contained. He said it like it was supposed to be reassuring, the kind of cancer you'd want if you had to have one. No chemo. Quick surgery. Manageable. Just a bump in the road; a lumpectomy surgery to remove it. That's how he framed it, and I wanted to believe him. I really did.

After the call, I didn't cry right away. I went into planning mode, like I always do. I compartmentalized. I put the information in a mental box and told myself I'd deal with it later. I didn't want to ruin the trip for Jenni. She had no idea so I smiled, reapplied my lipstick, and pretended everything was fine. When I needed a minute, I'd step into the bathroom, let out a few tears, then wipe them away and walk back out like nothing had happened. But eventually, one of the girls noticed. She pulled me aside. "You're not yourself," she said. And she was right, I wasn't. I broke down in front of her. I made her promise not to tell Jenni, at least not yet. I needed to make it through the trip.

Eventually, Jenni figured it out. She knows me too well and could sense something was off; the shift in my energy, the way I was holding it together too tightly, the moments I'd drift off into my own thoughts. I couldn't hide it from her anymore, so I finally told her. I took a breath and said, "I have breast cancer, but it's early, and I'm going to be okay." The words felt foreign coming out of my mouth, like I was saying them for someone else. I wanted to believe them, and maybe a part of me did, but another part of me was just trying to survive the moment. She didn't panic. She didn't cry. She just nodded softly, almost as if to say, *we'll get through this.* And from that point forward, we decided to take it one day at a time, no drama, no over-talking, just presence.

The rest of the trip shifted after that. It was still beautiful, still filled with laughter and celebration, but the lightness had changed. We went through the motions, the scouting, the meals, the photo ops, but there was a quietness behind everything now. This trip was supposed to be one of those memory-book moments, but it had turned into something else. Jenni didn't treat me any differently, though. She didn't flood me with pity or force me to talk about it. She just stood next to me in silence when I needed it. That's what real friends do. They hold a safe space.

When I look back on that trip, it still feels surreal. I was in one of the most beautiful places in the world, surrounded by joy, love, and sunlight, and yet inside I was unraveling. There was nothing I could style, plan, or manage my way through this time. I had spent my whole life creating flawless moments for everyone else, anticipating every problem before it happened, and fixing everything before anyone even noticed. But this was something I couldn't fix alone. This moment had shown up without warning, without design, and without my permission. Sometimes, even paradise gets interrupted.

**GUERDY IN ST. BARTS WHERE SHE FOUND OUT
SHE HAD BREAST CANCER, 2023**

Chapter 14

BOXED IN

When I got back to Miami, I scheduled the follow-ups like a good patient. I even remember thinking, just like the doctor said; "a small bump in the road", nothing big. I had spent my entire life being in control of my brand, my body, my schedule, my household and my emotions. Now I was being told I'd need to surrender all of that in exchange for a treatment plan that felt like someone else's checklist. I was used to designing events, not being designed by doctors. Each step of the process made me feel smaller. Every scan, every signature on a consent form, every time I changed into a paper gown while someone else held my chart, it chipped away at something I couldn't name. I wasn't in charge anymore, and that loss of power terrified me.

Time, which had always bent to my will, now belonged to appointments, labs, and second opinions. I tried to hold on to routines by sending emails in waiting rooms, taking calls in hospital parking lots, and pretending this was just another project to manage. But deep down, I knew this wasn't a detour, it was a new road entirely. I just didn't know where it was leading. The truth is, I don't remember a lot of that time clearly. I moved through those appointments like a ghost version of myself; present, but not there. Nurses would explain something, and I'd nod, hearing words but not their meaning. I was numb and in shock, and all the precision that once defined me disappeared overnight.

Russell became my note taker, my translator, and my force. He wrote everything down while I sat beside him, staring at the floor, waiting for the room to stop spinning. Russell snapped into first responder mode. He didn't flinch, didn't hesitate, he just handled it. While I sat frozen, he asked the right questions, got the information, and stayed grounded. It's like he knew I couldn't, so he did it for both of us. The irony wasn't lost on me, the planner who once orchestrated hundreds of moving parts suddenly couldn't plan her own next step. I went from being the driver of my life to being the passenger. Was I grateful to be Stage 0? Yes. But psychologically, it was still the C-word. People knew the word, but not its weight. I wasn't running my life anymore; I was being carried through it.

There were days when I'd sit in the car outside my house with the engine off, hands gripping the steering wheel, not ready to walk in. Not ready to answer medical history or genetic testing questions I didn't have answers to. Not ready to be "mom" or "babe" or "boss." I wasn't ready to be anything but scared. And I was scared. Even when I told family members who were calling from all over the world, checking in on me, "It's early, so I'm lucky." I tried to keep things clinical, logical, factual. But emotionally, I felt trapped. Part of me was scared to even tell my mother, who had already lost my brother and two of her granddaughters, because I knew she would think the worst. This would hurt her beyond belief, to know another of her children could be at great risk. She exaggerated everything; it's a Haitian trait, and that burden of emotionally containing myself to protect everyone else boxed me in even more. When I finally told her, there was silence at first, then it began. "Jésus!" she cried, her voice cracking through the phone so loud it felt like it echoed through the walls. I could hear her praying, pacing, calling out to the Lord as if they might get an answer right then and there. Between the sobs came that wail only a Haitian mother can make, the kind that sends panic through the whole house, pulling everyone into her grief whether they're ready or not. It was love, but it was chaos, and even from miles away I could feel the anxiety spread.

I remember standing in front of the mirror, looking at my breast after one of the pre-surgical consultations, disoriented. The room felt too bright, the mirror too honest. My reflection looked like me but didn't feel like me. What people rarely talk about is how much meaning lives inside that part of a woman's body. From the time we're teenagers, we're taught that breasts symbolize confidence, desirability, and even womanhood itself. They're dressed up, pushed up, measured, compared, and complimented, and somewhere along the way, they stop being just anatomy. They become part of your identity. So, when you're told that part of you might be cut, reshaped, or altered, it does something to your psyche. My mind raced between gratitude and grief. I told myself, It's just tissue. But emotionally, it wasn't that simple. I wasn't mourning vanity, I was mourning the part of myself that had carried me through every phase of womanhood; nursing my babies, dressing with confidence, and expressing intimacy with Russell. That part of me had always represented strength, beauty, and belonging. For the first time, I wondered what it would mean to still be me without the symmetry, and without the certainty. For a moment, I wondered if

I'd feel like damaged goods and no longer the same. That thought alone scared me.

But even in that moment of grief, I felt a quiet sense of gratitude. I never once asked God, "Why me?" Not once. Instead, I said, "Thank you." "Thank you that it wasn't worse. Thank you that it was caught it early." I thought of the women facing double mastectomies, the women living with Stage Four diagnoses, the ones praying just for more time, and here I was, mourning a small lumpectomy. The guilt hit me hard, especially when I was sitting in the oncology center's waiting room, looking around at other patients who I could tell were fighting for their lives. How dare I feel this broken when others would give anything to be in my position? Gratitude and guilt lived side by side in me, and that duality became its own silent ache.

That's the lie high-functioning women tell ourselves; that being prepared means being protected. I had planned my life with precision. I had done the work. I had checked every box. But now, life was boxing me in. Everywhere I turned, there were limitations. I couldn't book events too far out. I couldn't commit to speaking gigs or guarantee my availability. And I hated that. I hated saying "I don't know." I hated rescheduling. I hated being vague. But most of all, I hated not feeling like me. I was boxed in.

It reminded me of being back on the floor beside my grandmother in France; the same stillness, the same smallness. Back then, I sat quietly, waiting for someone to notice I was there. Now I was doing the same thing all over again, boxed in by fear instead of walls, waiting for someone to explain what was happening. The silence around me felt heavy, almost familiar, but this time it wasn't comforting, it was suffocating. I kept telling myself this was manageable. I'd get through the lumpectomy, heal, and move on. I held on to that thought like oxygen, convincing myself that I was nearing the end of something, not the start.

But just when I started to believe it, the results of the additional tests came in, and everything I'd believed was contained, came undone. The bump in the road became a collision course with a devastating new reality, one I wasn't prepared to face.

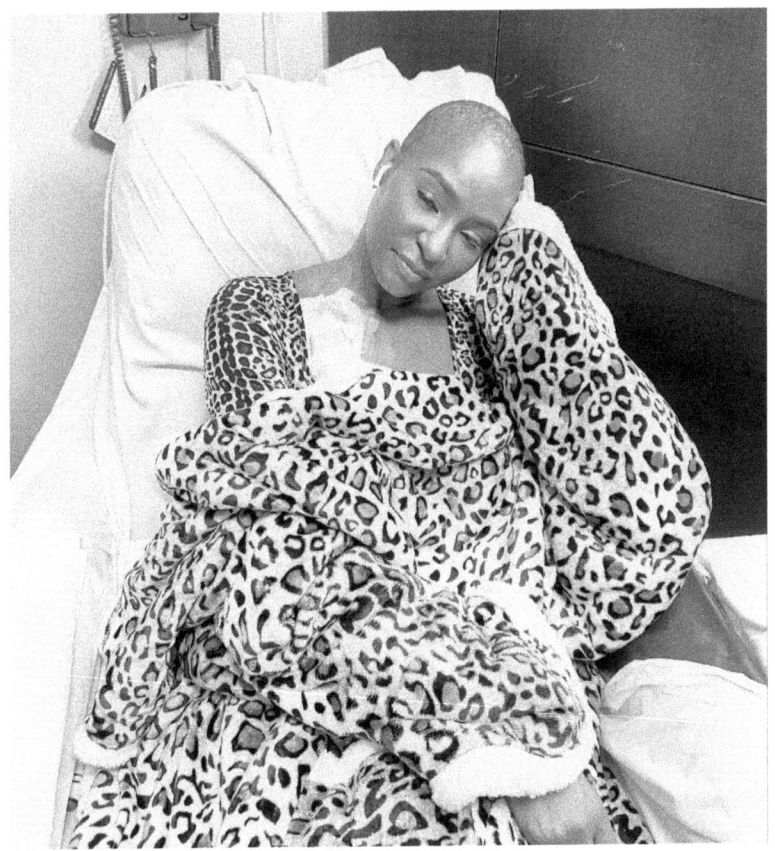

GUERDY DURING CANCER TREATMENT, 2023

Chapter 15

FIGHTING WITHOUT ARMOR

The new test results left no gray area. What had seemed straightforward at first was now something far more serious. An MRI revealed another tumor hiding behind the original Stage 0 DCIS. Two separate growths, not one. The first was still classified as DCIS, meaning the cancer cells were trapped inside the milk ducts and hadn't yet broken out. That was the one everyone had called "the good kind,"; the non-invasive kind that made it sound like I'd caught it early enough to stay calm. But the new tumor told a different story. It was invasive, Stage 1B, and estrogen-receptor positive; terms that meant the cancer was active and required a full treatment plan. My doctors immediately ordered several more tests and procedures. I took a genetic test which ruled out any inherited gene mutations which would increase the risk of breast cancer. I also underwent a biopsy of the new tumor and associated lymph node to determine whether it had spread. The lymph nodes act like filters in the body's drainage system, catching abnormal cells before they can move to other organs. If cancer cells show up there, it means the disease has found a pathway to travel. When the results came back, my doctor explained that the tumor was indeed invasive but the cancer had most likely not spread beyond the breast. I felt two things at once: fear because the disease was real, and relief because it was still local. It was still fightable but the treatment plan was suddenly different. Along with the already required lumpectomy surgery, I would now be required to undergo radiation therapy as well.

A former friend of mine who had gone through breast cancer before, was facing a recurrence at the same time I was beginning my journey. If anyone knew how to deal with this, it would be her, I thought. She told me, "All you can do, with everything coming at you at once, is take it one minute, one hour, one day at a time." Once I got past the shock of my new diagnosis, after thinking this would be a quick and easy treatment plan based on the initial Stage 0 findings, I decided to take that advice and focus only on what was directly in front of me. So, with those results in hand and treatment plan determined, we moved forward with the lumpectomy surgery.

A lumpectomy is the procedure where the surgeon removes the tumor and a small amount of surrounding tissue, called the margins, to make sure all the cancer cells are gone. It's less drastic than a mastectomy, but it's still major surgery when it's happening to you. Some people choose to undergo mastectomies because of various different reasons including genetics and type of cancer. I decided to forgo a mastectomy because my risk factors did not make it a necessity and my surgical oncologist recommended the lumpectomy. During the procedure, they also removed several associated lymph nodes that were close to the cancerous cells, just as a precautionary measure, to ensure that nothing had started to spread beyond the breast. My surgery was performed June 1, 2023. I went in trying to stay calm and focused on the process. When I woke up afterward, my surgeon seemed confident that the margins were clear and everything went smoothly. At that moment, I let myself believe it was over. I had done my part. The cancer was out, and I was ready to go home, recover in bed, and move on to the next item on our treatment check list: radiation. But a few days later, the pathology report came back with a different story. The margins weren't clean after all. That meant microscopic cancer cells were still present along the edges of the removed tissue, and we'd have to go back in to clear the margins. When I got that call, I was devastated. It felt like the floor dropped beneath me. I had convinced myself this first step would be the easiest part of the journey. Instead, the complications began from the start. It felt like being pushed onto a roller coaster I hadn't agreed to ride. That moment marked the start of what would become the emotional whiplash of my entire cancer journey; hope, then setback, relief, then dread; all within days.

After that first surgery, my doctors sent the tumor tissue out for what is called an Oncotype DX test; a genomic test that analyzes how a tumor behaves and predicts the likelihood of recurrence. When the results came back, my score was 29, which put me in the high-risk category. My doctor explained it in plain language; if I did surgery alone, my recurrence risk over the next ten years was about 36 percent. If I added hormone therapy, it could drop to roughly 20 percent. But if I completed the full plan which included surgery, hormone therapy, radiation, and now, chemotherapy; my recurrence risk would fall to about 9 percent. The difference between those numbers was a reminder that even the best odds still came with risk. Even at nine percent, the possibility of cancer's return lingered like a shadow I could never fully escape. Up until this point, the one bright spot that I was able to point to was the fact that chemotherapy was not included in my treatment plan. My DX score destroyed that perceived blessing and put me in a state of panic. However, after coming to grips with the reality of the situation, I knew it was the lesser of two evils, and that had to be enough. I didn't need to think twice, I told my doctor, "We're doing everything."

The second lumpectomy went smoothly, and this time, the cancerous margins were successfully cleared. When I got in the car to go home after surgery, still pretty groggy from the medicine, the first song I remember hearing was *'Scar Tissue'* by the Red Hot Chili Peppers, who happen to be mine and Russell's favorite group. The universe clearly has a sense of humor, because that's exactly what I was driving away with, scar tissue.

By the time I healed enough to lift my arms and move without aching, I knew what was next, the other c-word: chemotherapy. The word alone carried its own kind of weight. Surgery had felt like a fight I could see; something tangible, something to remove. But chemo was different. It meant surrendering my body to a chemical storm I couldn't control, and for someone like me, who built a life around control, that was its own kind of terror.

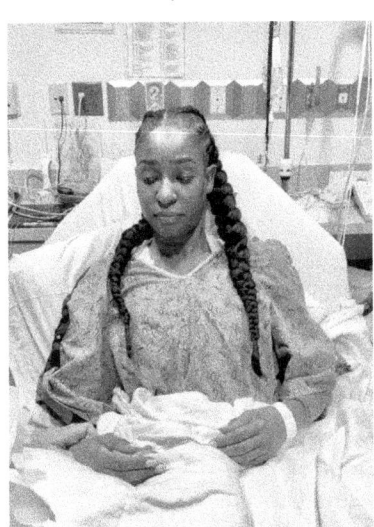
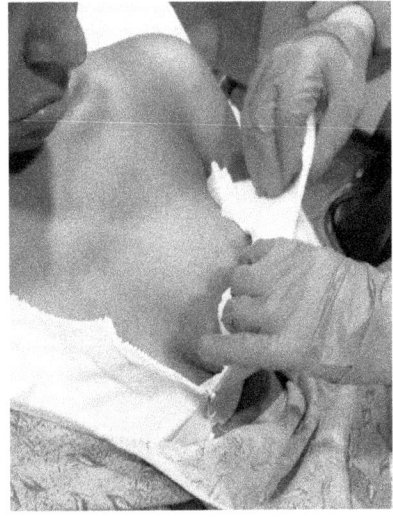

GUERDY AFTER LUMPECTOMY SURGERY, 2023

Chapter 16

THE OTHER C-WORD

The C word has a power all of its own. It's the word no one wants to hear; the one that follows you like an echo long before it ever becomes yours. People say "cancer" in hushed tones, but it's the other C-word that carries a different kind of weight. You grow up hearing that it's hard, that it takes everything out of you, that it leaves you unrecognizable, but you don't really know what that means until you have to go through it yourself. Chemotherapy wasn't like surgery, which had a clear beginning and end. It wasn't something that could be planned, executed, and checked off a list. It was an open-ended journey and something that would ask more of me than I'd ever been forced to give. It all still felt like a distant concept until the day I walked into my first consultation, and that's when the myth of it started turning into reality. The nurse spoke gently as she went through the details. Russell sat beside me, listening carefully as the nurse went over the medications, side effects, and scheduling. I only joined the conversation when she turned to me to ask how I preferred the chemotherapy to be administered. I honestly didn't know I had a choice, I thought they would just tell me what to do, the way they had every other time. So, I perked up when I realized I actually had a decision to make, finally.

She explained that she normally wouldn't even offer the choice, but because my treatment plan included only four rounds, and because she recognized me from television, she thought it might make sense to discuss both options. I could tell the recognition had changed her tone just slightly; she was kind and professional, but there was a certain caution in her delivery. It wasn't arrogance on my part, it was simply the awareness that even here, in one of the most humbling places a person can sit, the dynamic shifted when people knew who I was. She described the port option as a small surgical implant beneath the skin near my collarbone that would make infusions easier. The intravenous option, on the other hand, would mean no permanent device or scar, just a new needle in my arm with every session. On paper it sounded like a small medical decision, but emotionally it felt much larger than that. For one, the fact that I was able to make a decision finally felt sort of freeing. Also, the port represented surrender, a physical reminder of what I was going through even after it was all said and done. It also meant another surgical procedure before the chemo could start. The IV felt temporary and something I could control and remove when it was over. Four rounds didn't feel worth the scar, I initially thought. So, I chose the IV. It felt like a smaller invasion, and in a process where everything else was being decided for me, it was one small way of saying, "I still get to choose." At the time, I was happy and convinced myself I'd made the smart call, not realizing what I was truly in for. I still don't know why they even let me have a say in it, but something tells me she was being kind and trying to make the process a little easier on me. Russell tells me that I was very "persuasive" in my efforts to avoid the port and that probably played into it as well. Still, four rounds sounded manageable. I'd endured pregnancies with one natural birth and one C-section so how bad could four chemo rounds really be? That confidence was part defiance and part denial, the kind of bravado you can only describe as "f*** around and find out." And chemo made sure I did. Chemo didn't need to say a word, it showed me exactly what that meant. When the first infusion day arrived, Russell came with me. Of course, the boys were in school. In the weeks leading up to that day, I had gone into full planner mode. By then, I was almost looking forward to chemo, not because I wanted it, but because it gave me something tangible to prepare for, an event of sorts. If I couldn't control the diagnosis, I could at least control the packing list. I created a checklist that could rival any production prep sheet I'd ever written. Soft blanket? Check. Fuzzy socks? Check. Noise-canceling headphones, a satin pillowcase, a neck pillow, electrolyte packets, ginger candies, protein bars, my iPad loaded with shows, plus sanitizer wipes and a full-size blanket liner to lay over the leather recliner before I sat down, determined not to leave the chemo center with more germs than I came in with, check! My mask was in place, my cold socks and mittens were ready to chill my hands and feet to help prevent neuropathy (nerve damage that causes permanent tingling, pain, or numbness), and my tripod was packed so I could document everything, because in my head, this was going to be part of my next project; the YouTube channel I thought I was about to launch.

 Somewhere between the list-making and the Amazon deliveries, I started behaving like a seasoned pro before I'd even sat in the chair. I shared little snippets with my followers, talking about what I was packing, showing my essentials, giving advice as if I were a chemo influencer. It was my way of taking back control, of turning fear into something familiar, something manageable. I treated it like a production, a project, an event I could design my way through.

But what I didn't realize then was that this was not an event I could plan my way out of. There was no call sheet, no timeline, no crew to help clean up the mess. Chemo was about to hand me the humbling pill, or should I say, the allergic-reaction shock, that would strip away all that illusion of preparedness in one heartbeat.

The infusion center looked nothing like I'd imagined; rows of recliners lined up like an airplane cabin, each one facing the same direction. I was assigned a nurse named Marie, a fellow Haitian whose voice carried the same rhythm as home. That small familiarity grounded me instantly. We laughed as she noticed the frozen gloves and booties I'd brought along, the ones meant to protect my nails and nerves. "Ou pare tankou w'ap nan New York an janvye," she joked, "you're dressed like it's January in New York." For a moment, it almost felt normal.

Once I was settled in, the nurse gave me a quick rundown of what to expect. She explained the medications, the order they'd be administered, and mentioned that I'd first receive a dose of Benadryl to help prevent allergic reactions. I nodded, trying to take it all in as she hooked up the IV line. The IV slid into place easily. The machine began its soft rhythmic hum. I leaned back, forcing myself to relax. For a few minutes, everything felt fine, until it wasn't. My throat began to tighten, the air in my chest grew hot, and my vision started to blur. A sudden wave of pressure ran through me, and before I could process what was happening, the infusion center lit up in flashing lights and alarms. Marie's voice cut through the noise as she called for help, her calm turning sharp. Nurses rushed in from every direction. One shouted, "Stop the drip!" another grabbed oxygen.

That was my initiation into chemo. Not slow. Not gentle. Straight into chaos. Later, I learned the official name for what happened: an acute infusion reaction with extravasation. In plain terms, the drip was too fast and too sudden for my body to handle, and the medication leaked out of my vein, searing the tissue as it spread. When it was finally under control, I looked down to see a dark red trail running down my forearm. Because I'd chosen the IV, the medication had leaked through the vein, leaving a burn that would need lots of Bio-Oil and a year and a half to heal. Even now, the faint scar runs like a watermark across my skin, a small reminder of that naïve decision. I'd tried to avoid a scar and earned one anyway. After that incident, we continued and completed that chemo round. It took double the usual average time due to my body's sensitivity to the drug. Russell had to pop out to go get the boys. I told him to drop them home and then to come back because I didn't want them to see me weak and in distress. Needless to say, after this first round, we had to come up with a new plan. We'd need to place a port for the remaining three chemo rounds which meant, of course, another unexpected pop-up surgery, one more scar, one more reminder, and one more lesson in surrender.

When we got home, I went straight to the shower. I didn't want the boys to see me distraught after what had just happened. I didn't want to worry them or have to explain why their mother, who always held it together, suddenly couldn't. I stood there longer than usual, trying to wash off the smell of antiseptic and hospital air, almost as if I could rinse the whole experience away. Then I went straight to bed. The first couple of days after that infusion were manageable. As long as I stayed ahead of the nausea with my medication, I could function. I ate lightly, rested, checked emails, even convinced myself that maybe this was something I could handle.

The day after my chemo round, it was time for the Neulasta shot; a medication meant to help boost white blood cells and protect against infection. We were given the option to have Russell administer the injection at home instead of returning to the hospital, because Russell is a paramedic. It made the process more convenient; one less trip, one less sterile waiting room; but it didn't make it any easier. The shot burned going in, and at first, I thought that would be the worst of it. But about two days later, the real pain started. It crept in quietly, then spread everywhere. It was deep, splitting, and relentless; like my skeleton was cracking from the inside. Even the smallest movement sent shocks through my body. Russell had to help me walk to the bathroom because I couldn't stand up straight on my own. My body stiffened and jerked with every step; I felt like one of the dancers in the *Thriller* video; every movement fractured and mechanical, as if my bones were breaking with each shift of weight.

After that first round of chemo, I started to recognize the rhythm of it all. Every three weeks, the cycle reset. The first two days were tolerable, manageable even. Then the Neulasta pain came, followed by the physical crash, days of fatigue, nausea, and bone-deep exhaustion. Around day ten, I'd start to feel like myself again, just long enough to take a deep breath before the next round began. On the days I looked alive again, I'd post a photo or respond to a few messages, trying to project some kind of normalcy. I didn't want pity, there was no reason for people to see me crying through the pain. I'd already shared enough of my journey publicly, and watching me physically suffer would've been too much for others to witness, just as it already was for me to endure. To people watching, it might have looked inconsistent or even dramatic; one week in almost complete silence, the next suddenly full of energy. But, that was the pattern; disappear, resurface, disappear again. Life condensed into cycles of retreat and return.

And then there was chemo brain, the invisible side effect no one warns you about. It crept in quietly, stealing words mid-sentence, and making me forget what I'd walked into a room to do. For someone who has built a life on precision, detail, and planning, it was disorienting and extremely frustrating. I could design a wedding for hundreds of people down to the second, yet I'd stand in my kitchen staring at an open cabinet, unsure what I'd been looking for. Experiencing memory loss felt like little pieces of me floating away.

Chemo humbled me. It stripped away every illusion of control I had because I couldn't schedule it out of existence. I couldn't design my way through it. I couldn't delegate the suffering. It demanded total surrender. By the time the fourth round ended, I was hollowed out but grateful. I'd made it through and just as I let myself exhale, thinking I'd finally reached the end, the next phase waited quietly on the horizon: radiation.

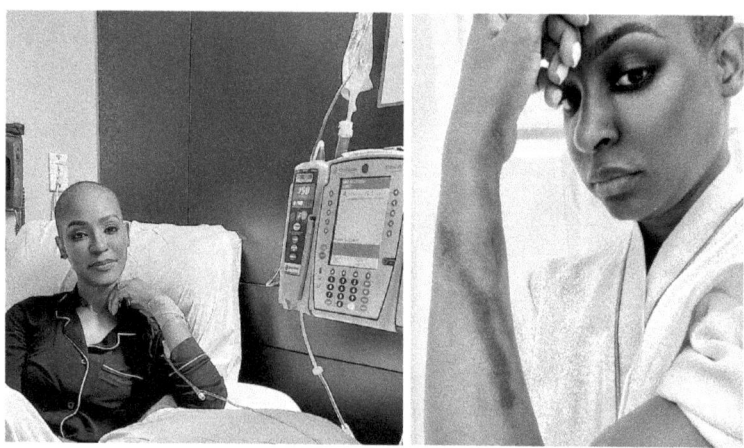

GUERDY AFTER FIRST ROUND OF CHEMO THROUGH THE VEIN (ROUND 1), 2023

Chapter 17
RADIATING

When chemo finally ended, I knew the hardest part was behind me. Radiation, they said, would be easier; more routine and less chaos. They were right. After everything I'd just survived, twenty short sessions sounded almost like recovery disguised as treatment. This time, I wasn't bracing for battle. I was preparing for maintenance. Compared to the unpredictability of chemo, radiation felt like structure: twenty sessions, Monday through Friday, at the same time each day. It became my new routine, the kind that didn't demand courage so much as consistency.

Before my first appointment, I did what most of us do these days, I went online. I wanted to see what the process looked like, what kind of scarring to expect, and how my skin might react. The search results were shocking; full of extreme cases that looked nothing like what I'd been told to expect. The images showed open wounds and burns far beyond what was typical. Even more discouraging, almost none of them reflected women of color. I scrolled through page after page of fair skin and pink undertones, looking for something, anything that looked like me. There wasn't one. I closed the laptop with more questions than answers.

When I met with my radiologist, I showed him the photos. He smiled kindly and said, "Please ignore those. Everyone's skin is different, and yours will heal in its own way." I appreciated his reassurance, but it made me think. If everyone's skin is different, why wasn't everyone represented? Why was there not a single image of what radiation looks like on deeper tones, or any real variety at all? In the waiting room, I spoke with two other women, one Latina, another Asian who said they'd also searched online and found nothing that resembled their skin. It wasn't just a Black woman's issue; it was a human one. So many of us were navigating this process without a visual map that reflected who we were.

That realization hit me harder than I expected. I began to understand how much of medicine, like most things, is built around what's been studied and shown the most. It wasn't anyone's fault; it just made me realize how much room there is to include everyone's experience. I was grateful for my care team, they guided me with compassion, but I also hoped that someday, others like me could find more images and examples that reflected them too. The truth is, not everybody reacts the same, not every recovery looks the same, and yet the information given to patients rarely reflects that range. Those gaps shape everything, from diagnosis to treatment, to survival. I later learned that minorities are about 45% more likely to die from breast cancer than white women, despite developing it at similar rates. The gap isn't about biology alone, it's about access, awareness, and bias that runs deep. Too often, minorities' pain is dismissed, symptoms questioned, and outcomes predetermined by a system that doesn't fully see them.

Even the breast cancer screening guidelines were limited from what I read. Minorities are more likely to develop aggressive, fast-moving forms like triple-negative breast cancer, yet they're encouraged to start mammograms at the same age as everyone else. For many, that delay costs precious time. They're underrepresented in clinical trials, so the drugs that save lives often aren't studied on their bodies in the first place. Many are treated at underfunded hospitals, have less access to specialists, and face more insurance barriers that delay care. That's when I realized representation is about inclusion. When people don't see themselves reflected in the process, they're less likely to trust it. They might skip appointments, stop treatment early, or assume the system was never built for them in the first place. That lack of visibility is cultural and generational; a silent gap that costs lives.

It was a lot to think about, but once I began radiation, my world became smaller, one appointment at a time, one day at a time, one breath at a time. Inside the treatment room, the technicians spoke in precise measurements. They permanently tattooed tiny dots on my skin, markers for where the beams would meet. Technically, I have tattoos now. I used to agree with Kim Kardashian when she said, *"you don't put a bumper sticker on a Bentley."* Well, life had other plans for me. I lay on the cold table with my arms raised above my head, the position both vulnerable and defiant. Once they left the room and the door sealed, the silence grew heavy. A red light blinked. The machine rotated slowly, humming its sterile lullaby. I could feel the vibration in my ribs even though the beam itself was invisible. I learned to hold my breath for five seconds, then ten, waiting for the hum to stop.

Radiation affected more than my skin. It changed my taste buds. Everything I ate started to taste flat, metallic, or just...off. Russell would experiment with seasonings, trying to find combinations that might wake my taste-buds; extra citrus, a little more salt, anything to make food feel like something to look forward to again. He never complained, never made it about him. He just adjusted, quietly, the way he always does.

At first, the skin where they targeted me looked untouched. By the second week, it darkened, gray to deep brown. The burns appeared on my left side, covering half my upper torso. The demarcation was so distinct that I couldn't wear anything revealing, and even if I wanted to, I had to keep it covered at all times to protect it from the sun. I became addicted to my Bio-Oil, Haitian castor oil, and Aquaphor; my little trio of comfort. I'd layer them gently, hoping to soothe the itchiness and bring some balance back to my skin. Russell came with me to every single appointment. He'd wait in the lobby with a book or his phone, never once complaining about the hours. Sometimes he'd walk me to the door of the treatment room, squeeze my hand, and whisper, "See you on the other side." He never left my side, not once. Knowing he was out there, just beyond the wall, made the sterile room feel less lonely. Each session ended the same; the machine fell silent, the door opened, and a nurse said, "You're all done for today, Ms. Abraira." I'd nod, thank her, pull my sweater over the gown lines, and walk outside into that Miami sunshine, blinking like someone returning from another planet.

In the end, that experience taught me that this was bigger than me. It wasn't just about healing my body; it was about understanding the larger system that so often fails women who look like me. Radiation exposed more than cancer cells; it exposed the cracks in care, in representation, and in how we define survivorship. That's why I chose to share my journey openly, even when it was uncomfortable. Because someone, somewhere, needed to see what it looked like on us. But we'll get to that part later, when the cameras start rolling.

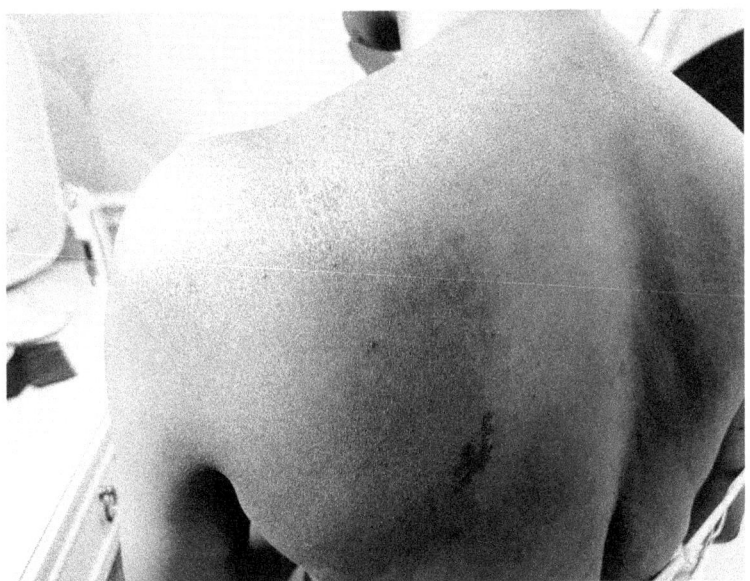

GUERDY'S RADIATION BURNS TO CHEST & BACK, 2023

GUERDY RINGING THE RADIATION BELL, 2023

Chapter 18
THE RECONSTRUCTION ERA

Before addressing the reconstruction of my breasts after radiation, I had to undergo a full hysterectomy, removing my uterus, ovaries, and fallopian tubes, to reduce my body's overall hormone supply and lower my risk of recurrence. That procedure marked another major turning point in my survivorship plan. It was medically straightforward but emotionally layered. The surgery represented finality; not just physically, but symbolically too. I didn't anticipate how much it would affect me until afterward. I will never be able to have another child, and while I wasn't planning to, the permanence of that reality carried its own quiet grief. It wasn't about wanting more children, it was about losing the option. The awareness surfaced in unexpected moments, like seeing a newborn at the grocery store or hearing a friend talk about pregnancy. I understood why it had to be done, but there was still a strange sadness in watching my body be redesigned for survival. The hysterectomy had been about prevention. The next surgery would be about restoration.

After radiation, my left breast began to change in ways that I could not ignore; just as my doctor had warned could happen. Not only did the coloration of my skin in the radiated areas darken drastically; the tissue started tightening and shrinking, pulling against my skin as though it was retreating inward. It was one of the side effects they tell you to expect, but nothing prepares you for how it actually feels when it's your own body changing before your eyes. What began as a dull soreness evolved into a deep, pinching, ache that made everyday movement feel like labor. Lifting my arm became nearly impossible without dropping whatever I was holding. That's when I knew I had developed a capsular contracture; a condition where scar tissue forms around an implant and hardens, squeezing it like a fist. It didn't just hurt; it restricted me. I could no longer lift my arm past a certain point, and that limitation was not only frustrating but frightening. After everything I had already endured, my body was once again dictating what I could and couldn't do.

The pain and tightness weren't just surface issues, they began to affect my entire upper body. The muscles around my shoulder weakened from disuse, and the stiffness from radiation only made it worse. I eventually started physical rehab because I had lost so much strength and mobility. The sessions were painful but necessary. Each small gain; raising my arm a little higher, holding a light weight for a few seconds longer, felt monumental. As the weeks passed, it became clear to me that the implants had to go. My surgeon explained that I had the option to remove and replace them but also warned that even with replacements, I might need up to two additional surgeries before they would look symmetrical. Even then, it wasn't guaranteed. I didn't want to risk more complications and didn't want to become a slave to more procedures and recovery periods, so, I chose the easier, cleaner road, and decided not to replace them and go au naturel. And so, the plan was made, I would remove both implants and rebuild using fat grafting. After that, I would get a Renuvion procedure with the plastic surgeon who originally did my implants after Liam was born. He specialized in this technology which would tighten the loose skin under my arms and back that was left behind from the implant removal. But first, I needed to tackle the reconstructive surgery process handled by my breast reconstructive surgeon.

My breast reconstructive surgeon explained that my own fat would be processed and injected to restore volume after the implants were removed. The fat was taken from my flanks and my back, a sort of internal exchange. If there was one silver lining, it was that there was plenty of fat to work with, thanks to the thirty pounds I'd gained from steroids, medication, and weeks of being stuck in bed. I even joked with my surgeon that at least I'd be getting an hourglass shape-ish out of the deal. It was the kind of humor that helped me get through it, finding light in the middle of something that felt so heavy.

The breast reconstructive surgery itself went as planned, but the aftermath brought a different kind of challenge. I have always been keloid-prone; my body's way of healing is to overdo it. My scars rise, thicken, and itch long after they're supposed to settle. Before reconstruction, I told my surgeon about this over and over. "I keloid easily," I said. "Please be careful." I showed him my port scar, already raised and shiny. "This is how my body heals." He nodded and said he'd use a special closure technique, and assured me it would be fine. But that familiar "doctor knows best" energy filled the room, the kind that politely brushes off a patient's lived truth.

Weeks after successful reconstructive surgery, I started to feel it: the unmistakable tightness beneath the skin, along with the itching, and the raised ridge forming where the incision had been. I knew immediately what was happening. When my surgeon examined me, he tried to reframe it: "They're hypertrophic scars, not true keloids," he said, emphasizing the difference as though it might make me feel better. I just smiled and said, "Well, to me it's a keloid. You can call it a hypertrophic scar if you want, it's all the same to me. Toma-to, to-mato." He laughed, and so did I, but my humor was covering pain. Because I didn't care what it was called, I just wanted relief. The scars were thick, raised, and angry, exactly as I warned they would be.

The scar that ran about four to five inches underneath my right breast, precisely along the bra-line, was getting much worse. Then the pain turned from annoying to unbearable. What began as a burning sensation evolved into something deeper: a pulsing, searing, electric pain that radiated with every breath. It felt as though fire lived beneath my skin. The lightest touch of fabric against it made me wince. I couldn't wear normal clothes; even the seam of a tank top was too much. I ended up cutting away half of the breast area of my tank tops just to let the scar breathe. The friction was torture. The area stayed inflamed, red, and hot to the touch. At night, the throbbing kept me awake. It was as though my chest had a heartbeat of its own.

I told my surgeon that something wasn't right. He told me to "wait it out." He said it might calm down on its own. But my instincts screamed otherwise. I had lived in this pain every single day. I knew my body, and I knew that this wasn't "normal healing." Still, I was told to wait. For three months, I lived with a burning, pulsating wound, trying to pretend it was improving when deep down I knew it was worsening. Several times, I tried steroid injections directly into the scar; an extremely painful procedure that had actually helped some of my previous scars from other procedures. However, with this scar, I only received minimal and temporary relief. By the time he agreed that it needed surgical revision, I was emotionally and physically exhausted. I had been in agony for months because I had been told to be patient instead of being believed.

During one of my follow-up appointments with my radiologist for my upper arm mobility issues, I had a conversation that changed everything. While checking in on how my arm was recovering, he mentioned in passing a treatment I had never heard of: Superficial Radiation Therapy (SRT). It's a form of low-dose radiation used to prevent or treat keloids. I asked him to explain it further, and that's when he said something that stopped me cold; that it had always been an option for someone like me. I remember feeling a wave of frustration rise up in my chest. I told him that I had warned my reconstructive surgeon repeatedly about being keloid-prone, and yet SRT had never been offered to me. The radiologist looked almost apologetic. I could tell he was surprised, too. I left that appointment angry, not just because I had to go through unnecessary pain, but because the information was there all along. My reconstructive surgeon simply hadn't thought to mention it.

The irony was that my left breast, the one that had been radiated, healed beautifully. Smooth, clean, barely a mark left behind. At first, it didn't make sense. The breast that had gone through twenty rounds of radiation, the one everyone warned would have trouble healing, was flawless. But, when I learned more, it clicked; the radiation that had once been used to destroy cancer cells had also suppressed the overproduction of collagen in the scar tissue. In simple terms, the radiation that once hurt me actually helped me heal. Meanwhile, the right breast, the one that hadn't been radiated, did exactly what my body always does, which was develop a keloid. Just as it had with past surgeries and incisions. After all the pain and procedures, I ended up needing radiation again; this time on the "healthy" breast, to treat the very kind of scarring that the first radiation had unknowingly prevented. Talk about a full-circle moment. The same treatment that once terrified me had now become the thing that could give me relief. Still, I want to be clear, I genuinely liked my surgeon. He was skilled, kind, and had guided me through major stages of reconstruction with care. This wasn't about him being a "bad doctor." This was about a learning curve for both of us. For him, it was understanding that my body doesn't follow the textbook. For me, it was realizing that even the best doctor in the world can miss something if they're not living in your skin.

Ultimately, my surgeon had to first re-excise and remove the problematic scars. Once he re-sutured the wound, and I was awake from the anesthesia, Russell had to bring me directly to the radiation center for my initial SRT treatment to prevent new keloids from forming. I would have to go back three more times to complete the treatment. The treatment also covered my hysterectomy scars. Those earlier incisions had developed the same raised, tight bands, and treating them alongside my right breast felt like closing the loop on months of physical and emotional healing. It was the first time my recovery plan felt complete, addressing both the visible and hidden scars that told the story of everything my body had endured.

This preventable experience stayed with me. It wasn't just about the scars, it was about not being heard. I had been clear from the beginning; my body doesn't heal like everyone else's. I knew it, and I said it, but the people responsible for helping me heal chose not to believe me. I started documenting everything; photos, notes, the progression of scars, the days when movement hurt more than others. Patients live in their bodies full-time. Doctors only visit. And that was the moment I stepped into a new kind of role; advocate. Until then, I had assumed that if I showed up, followed orders, and asked questions, that was enough. But surviving cancer teaches you that passivity is not protection. You can do everything "right" and still get overlooked. Advocacy is about being present, in your own story, in your own body, in every single decision being made about it. I learned to come to appointments with notes and questions written out. I stopped apologizing for wanting explanations. I stopped shrinking myself to make providers comfortable. I learned to say, "I understand your perspective, but this is what I'm experiencing."

I also learned that advocating for yourself doesn't always mean fighting, it means insisting on partnership. It means reminding medical professionals that they are treating a person, not a project. It means asking, "What are all of my options?" and not being embarrassed to push back if something doesn't sound right. I began to realize how often women, especially women of color, are taught to downplay their pain, to be agreeable, to trust the process even when our instincts tell us something's wrong. Advocacy, for me, became a form of self-respect.

Advocacy also means that sometimes what's been "standard practice" for decades doesn't fit every woman. Medical experience doesn't make you infallible, it should make you curious. Doctors have to be willing to unlearn what they think they know and listen to the women in front of them, especially when our bodies don't follow the textbook. I'm not an exception; I'm simply proof that there's more than one way to heal. Don't wait for permission to protect your own body, because the truth is, no one is more invested in your healing than you are.

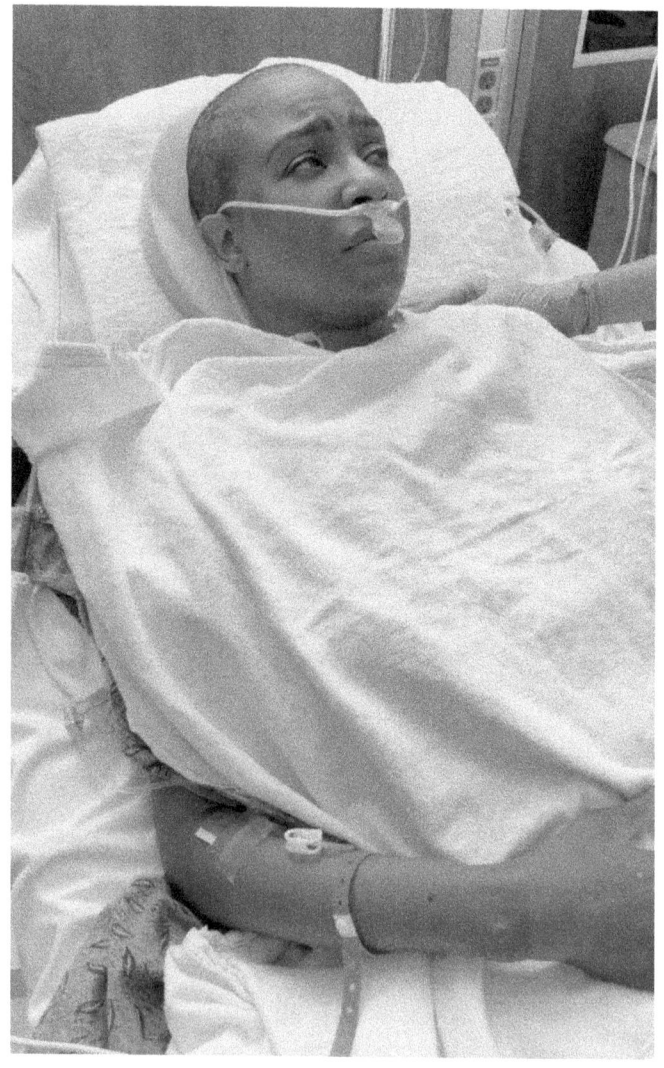

GUERDY AFTER ONE OF HER RECONSTRUCTIVE SURGERIES, 2024

Chapter 19

THE NEW NORMAL

It happened at BravoCon of all places. What's BravoCon, you ask? Well, it's the ultimate fan experience stemming from the popular Bravo TV network shows like the one I'm on, The Real Housewives of Miami. It's a place where thousands of Bravo fans get an opportunity to connect with their favorite Bravolebrities from every franchise under one roof to celebrate all things Bravo. From November 3–5, 2023, in Las Vegas, the convention center was buzzing with flashing cameras, endless selfies, and fans decked out in their favorite Housewives quotes on T-shirts. I was sitting on stage with my *Real Housewives of Miami* cast, doing what we do: giving the audience a good time. I hadn't planned to make any kind of official announcement, but even though my official ringing of the bell for my last radiation treatment was scheduled for November 8th, I had already been told by my oncologist that I was cancer-free. So, it felt right that during this panel, when asked about my health, I would share the good news. I said the first thing that came to mind; "I'm cancer-free." The audience clapped, cheered, and some even cried. When I looked over to my right, Marysol was teary-eyed, Adriana chimed in to give me strength, and Alexia reached over to touch my hand. Those were nice gestures from my castmates that I really appreciated at that moment; it showed genuine support. You wouldn't have thought I'd just dropped the biggest headline of the weekend, but within hours, the internet did what it does; it amplified. *"Guerdy Abraira Announces She's Officially Cancer-Free,"* the headlines read. The truth is, I didn't even think of it as an announcement. I was just repeating what my doctor had told me; that there were no traces of cancer left, meaning cancer-free, simple as that. That moment on stage was me sharing my relief in real time. Relief that the worst was behind me.

After seeing the media attention it got, I posted the announcement on my Instagram as soon as I had the chance; it was the next thing to do given how big of a deal it had become. As social media comments started rolling in after I posted that day, people were genuinely happy for me, flooding my post with congratulatory comments. But what was interesting was that a few got hung up on the wording: "Wait, is she cancer-free or in remission?" which created lots of layered conversation threads within my post. People chimed in about their take on whether I was cancer-free or in remission. "Does she even know the difference?" The truth? I didn't. This was my first time experiencing cancer, and I was learning as I went. When I looked it up later, the difference made sense, "cancer-free" means there's no evidence of disease in the body at that moment, while "remission" means the same thing but typically refers to staying that way over a longer period of time. So in my case, I was correct in saying "cancer-free," as it had just been told to me by my oncologist, and to be honest, I didn't care which way was considered correct; to survivors, it meant freedom and a chance to live again without that shadow constantly hovering.

What I didn't realize at the time was that being told you're cancer-free doesn't automatically mean you're free from everything that comes with it. People hear "cancer-free" and instantly go into celebration mode; smiles, hugs, and congratulations. It's almost like when someone at the office has a birthday. Everyone takes a quick five-minute break, gathers around the conference table, cuts the cake, sings happy birthday, and then goes right back to work. That's how people treat survivorship, like it's a quick moment of acknowledgment before returning to business as usual. *Cut the cake, clap it out, and carry on.*

For some people, especially those who only see glimpses of my life on TV, my cancer became a storyline they watched unfold for one season, as if it could be neatly resolved by the finale. They expected the next season to bring a whole new plot, like a quick home makeover episode on HGTV; fresh paint, new look, move on. And to be fair, I understand why. There's only so much that can be shown within an ensemble cast of nine women, where even the "friends of" have as much screen time as the main cast. So, the audience ends up seeing just a fraction of a much bigger story and assumes that when the cameras cut, the healing does too. But that's not how life works. Speaking of HGTV; before appearing on Real Housewives of Miami, I was on a HGTV special called Holiday Crafters Gone Wild. It was a fantastic experience where I met a lot of talented people and ultimately fell short in the friendly competition. I believe my teammate and I were too ambitious in our concept and fell short with the execution considering the limited time we had. In the end, there was some amazing talent there that executed better than us, but I had a great time and learned so much from the other contestants.

That kind of limited exposure also creates three very different versions of community outside of my real one. First, there are the people who knew me before television: friends, clients, and family who've seen the real me over decades. They know that what they see on-screen isn't always a full reflection of who I am, especially when certain interactions with other castmates are condensed into a few edited minutes. Still, even they can get influenced by the on-screen version of me and start to merge the two. Then, there are the complete strangers, the ones who only know me through the edit and who form strong opinions about who I am based solely on what made it to air. Both groups watch, react, and form opinions, most times without realizing how much was left unsaid. And then, there's the third group, the ones who are *me*. The ones who've walked through cancer themselves, who know what it feels like to wait for results or lose your hair or stare in the mirror not recognizing the person looking back. My connection with them has been the most special of all. Many have reached out to tell me that watching my journey encouraged them to schedule a mammogram or pushed them to seek answers they had been putting off. Some even said it saved their lives. That kind of connection; the kind that turns pain into purpose, goes far beyond what television can ever capture.

Still, purpose doesn't protect you from judgment. It's funny how people have such strong opinions about how I show up as a survivor after beating cancer. I've received many messages telling me to "put on a wig already," as if my shaved head makes others uncomfortable. Some even suggested the reason I kept it short was for attention. What they don't know is that I keep my hair shaved because of a daily pill called Anastrozole; a medication I'll be taking for the next five years. It works by blocking my body's ability to make estrogen, lowering my risk of recurrence. But like most things that save you, it comes with side effects. For me, it causes stiffness, joint pain, and a kind of fatigue that no amount of sleep can fix. It's also affected my hair growth; the hair around my temples hasn't filled in like the rest, which makes it look like I have a receding hairline when I try to grow it out. Let's just say Guerdy was giving Gérard vibes. That's why I keep it shaved low.

And while that's one visible reminder of what treatment left behind, others are felt more than seen. The hardest side effect to manage has been the hot flashes, and they don't discriminate. They show up anywhere, anytime, multiple times a day and night. One minute I'm fine, and the next it feels like a furnace has been lit inside me. This is also a major reason why I have kept my hair short. That's where Veozah comes in. It's a non-hormonal medication that helps manage the hot flashes and night sweats that come from menopause, or in my case, forced menopause. It doesn't erase them, but it turns the volume down enough for me to function. The irony is almost poetic, a kind of yin and yang in pill form; one turns up the fire, the other cools it down. Every day, I balance the two. Veozah lasts about seven hours, so I plan my doses like I plan events: strategically. If I take it in the morning, I can power through my day, but by nightfall, I'm sweating through the sheets. If I take it later, I can stay composed in the evening, but mornings feel like I'm walking through a heat wave. There's no perfect formula, only trade-offs. I joke that I'm like Cinderella when the clock strikes midnight and the magic fades. So, maybe one day in the near future, I'll feel comfortable enough to wear a wig again sometimes, if it's not too hot outside or if it's a special occasion. But, when I see those comments, I can't help but wonder, why can't people just be kind and mind their own business? Cancer isn't something I chose to have. Statistics show that one in eight women will develop breast cancer, and one in three people will be diagnosed with some form of cancer in their lifetime. The truth is, the chances of it being you are closer than you think. Extending empathy and kindness doesn't cost a dime.

As hurtful as these types of comments were, I made a conscious effort to try to ignore them and focus on me and my recovery, and in doing so, I realized healing isn't just about the physical part, it's about unpacking the mental and emotional baggage that comes with it. I started therapy for the first time because I wanted to confront everything cancer had shaken loose. Therapy wasn't just about processing what had happened to me physically, it was about giving myself a full reboot on life and my mindset. The diagnosis forced me to stop long enough to look at patterns I'd been carrying for decades. It made me see how much of my "strong-woman" energy had really been its own kind of survival mode in disguise. In those sessions, I started tracing my reactions all the way back to being nine years old and the day my brother and I were sent to Miami without our parents and left in a relative's house that never felt like home. I had spent my entire childhood wondering why it had to be us who were sent away. I always felt like I had done something wrong, like this was a punishment. That belief, that love could be conditional and that safety could be taken away, never really left me. It became part of my wiring.

When I got older, that wound evolved into overachievement. I wanted to be so good, so dependable, that no one would ever think to leave me behind again. But no amount of perfection could undo the ache that came from feeling unseen. My mother was loving in her own way; through duty, discipline and structure. So, I worked even harder to earn what I thought love was supposed to look like: approval. Looking back now, I understand that she pushed us out of love, not lack thereof. She believed opportunity was waiting for us, even if it meant sending us far away from her. Her way of loving was preparing us to survive anywhere.

That pattern followed me into my adult life. I poured myself into work, relationships, and motherhood, determined to prove I could handle anything and everything. Even when I was bullied in school for being different; my accent, my clothes, my Haitian background, I just smiled and adapted. I didn't know how to stop performing and projecting strength. I didn't know how to let people see me vulnerable. Therapy finally gave me the space to do that; to take off the armor I'd been wearing since childhood, and figure out who I was underneath it all.

Cancer doesn't just happen to one person; it happens to everyone under the same roof. We were all living with Post-Traumatic Stress Disorder. It wasn't just me. PTSD isn't always about flashbacks or panic after the crisis ends. For me, it showed up in ways I didn't expect: difficulty concentrating, restless nights, losing interest in activities I once loved, even event planning for a while. My nervous system was still on high alert, as if it hadn't gotten the memo that the danger was over.

For Russell, it looked different. As a fire captain, he's trained to react in emergencies; focused, efficient, calm. That instinct kicked in with my diagnosis, and he became the caretaker before he could process what that meant for him emotionally. He managed appointments, meds, meals, everything. He was incredible. But, when it was all over, turning off that caretaker switch was hard. I had to remind him gently that I needed my husband back, not my nurse. My sons, Miles and Liam, were 16 and 10 at the time while I was fighting cancer, and no matter how much I tried to shield them, they felt the energy shift. They saw the fear on days when I couldn't hide it. Each of us carried the trauma differently, and each of us had to find our own way to release it. Therapy became a family tool, not just mine; to help us name what we had all endured and learn how to live without waiting for the next alarm to go off. My boys, my beautiful boys who I call CareVivors, carried me through it all with a kind of love and strength that made every hard moment bearable.

Being "cancer-free" was never the end, it was the beginning of learning how to exist differently. The title of survivor doesn't mean you've outrun the fear; it means you've learned how to live beside it. I still go for my scans every six months, and the anxiety never fully disappears. But, in between those appointments, I live fully, intentionally, and with gratitude. I trust the science. I trust my faith. And most of all, I trust myself. Healing stopped being something I did after treatment and started becoming the way I live. I take twenty-three pills a day now; a mix of vitamins, supplements, and prescriptions that help my body recover, regulate, and protect itself. I cut out most processed foods and load up on cruciferous vegetables like broccoli, kale, bok choy, and cabbage. I added more greens and flaxseed and dialed back on soy, red meat, and alcohol. Before, I used to pour a glass of wine every night while I cooked; that was my wind-down ritual. Now, I rarely drink. If I do, it's when I'm out at an event or celebrating something special. When I'm home and not traveling for work, I rotate between simple, balanced meals, like Greek yogurt with fruit and keto granola or eggs for breakfast; Asian-style chicken salads with cruciferous vegetables for lunch and fish or chicken with veggies for dinner. I make cold-pressed juices with beets, apples, celery, carrots, pineapple, soursop, and ginger. My son Miles helps with meal prep. I jokingly call him my dietitian. He knows exactly what goes into everything, and he's proud of it. Those routines give me something medicine can't, a sense of normalcy.

So as the congratulations fade and people say, *"You beat cancer, now you can go back to normal,"* I've realized there is no going back. Everyone wants a neat ending, a full recovery, a version of you that fits who you were before, but that person no longer exists. Healing changes everything; how you see yourself, how you move through the world and what you give your energy to. The idea of "normal" becomes something you outgrow. What replaces it isn't perfect or predictable, but it's yours. It's quieter, more intentional, and more aware of how fragile and beautiful life really is. That's the new normal; living with purpose, on my own terms, with gratitude for every ordinary day that follows.

GUERDY AND HER FAMILY LAST DAY OF CHEMO, 2023

Chapter 20

ON CAMERA

When I decided to join The Real Housewives of Miami for its reboot in Season 4 a few years ago, I thought I knew what I was signing up for. The show had been off the air for years, and Bravo was bringing it back with a new cast meant to represent the modern Miami; successful, outspoken, multicultural women, balancing business, motherhood, and friendship under the same relentless spotlight. For me, it felt like an opportunity to show a fuller picture of success; family, faith, culture, and hard work, all coexisting in one life. I joined to share the world I had built with my husband, Russell, our sons, and the business that I had grown from the ground up. In fact, season 4 did feature me planning the wedding of a castmate, but unfortunately, life doesn't pause for television schedules. This was during the tail- end of the COVID pandemic and unfortunately the wedding had to be cancelled just a couple days prior due to the death of the bride's mother.

A couple seasons after, during season 6, when I heard the words "you have cancer," I was faced with a question far bigger than any storyline. Would I step away until I looked "put together" again, or would I keep the promise I made when I joined; to live my life authentically, no matter how imperfect it looked? In those first few weeks after my diagnosis, which was just a couple of weeks before filming, I found myself in a fog. Everything felt heavy and uncertain. I thought about walking away from the show and the cameras. But the more I sat with it, the clearer it became. When people later asked why I decided to share my cancer journey on camera, my answer came easily: "Why not?" I had opened the door to let people see my life; the good, the beautiful, the complicated. To suddenly hide would've felt dishonest, like choosing convenience over truth. Cancer was part of my story now, and I wasn't going to pretend it didn't exist just because it wasn't glamorous.

Still, it wasn't a decision I made lightly. I remember sitting at the kitchen island with Russell, the same table where we'd celebrated birthdays and solved crises. We didn't do much deliberation as the question for us was still, "why not film it, you will help people." That sentence settled something deep in me. It wasn't just about me anymore. Should anything happen to me, I wanted there to be a record; a love letter to the universe of how I fought, how I lived, and how we all got through it together. Not sharing felt selfish, like hiding behind comfort when transparency could save lives. I'd always said I wanted to be authentic on camera; this was the truest test of that promise.

Growing up, I'd seen how illness was treated as something to hide. In the Caribbean community and perhaps other cultural groups too, it seemed as though they fear gossip more than diagnosis. A neighbor would lose weight, and instead of asking if she was sick, folks would say, "She must be cursed." Silence was the norm, but silence kills. I've seen women delay screenings or skip treatments entirely because they were terrified of what others might think. The real danger isn't the disease, it's the stigma. I refused to feed that culture of hiding. If my openness could convince even one woman to schedule her mammogram, the discomfort of being vulnerable on television would be worth it. Those fears run deep in our communities. It breaks my heart when people treat science like the enemy of faith or tradition. In many cultures, illness is still viewed as something that can be prayed or detoxed away, as if medicine and miracles can't exist in the same sentence. But bringing science into those belief systems is critical. Faith and holistic care can absolutely be part of the healing journey, but they shouldn't replace medical treatment. My father is living proof of that balance. When he was diagnosed with prostate cancer, years before my diagnosis, he leaned on both his faith and his physicians. Prayer and treatment, he believed, worked hand in hand, alongside herbal remedies passed down from generation to generation. Science at the end is what saved him. Watching my father's strength taught me that faith and science can coexist and that healing takes both surrender and action. That belief was something I led with as I began stepping back into the public eye.

I had just started filming again, beginning to find my footing both on the show and in sharing my journey, when the first real test of my strength appeared, not in treatment, but in trust. During a vulnerable moment, I confided in a castmate about my diagnosis and told her to please not tell anyone as I was still processing it. At that point, I hadn't even told all my closest friends yet. I thought I had time. Since the show itself wouldn't air for at least six months after filming, I assumed I could move at my own pace and share the news when I was ready. So, when I later learned that this castmate immediately shared my diagnosis at an event at her house, with

On Camera

other castmates, and people I didn't even know, I was floored. I remember the moment it hit me; this was something deeply personal and private that I hadn't even had the chance to fully absorb myself, and now it was already in circulation. My biggest concern quickly became the possibility of it reaching the media before I was emotionally prepared to talk about it. I knew how easily a story like that could be told the wrong way, or sensationalized for headlines, and I didn't want that to happen.

So, within a few days, I released a statement publicly. I was forced to do it as an act of protection. I was trying to reclaim the news that was supposed to be mine; news that had already been taken from me. The response was immediate. Within minutes of posting, my phone was flooded with messages. The outpouring of love and support was massive. So many people were genuinely kind and uplifting, but it also felt suffocating. I wasn't ready to receive that kind of attention yet. I was still in the thick of processing my own emotions, and suddenly it felt like the whole world was processing them with me.

When I later confronted the person who had shared my diagnosis, the explanation shifted more than once. First, it was acknowledged that I had told her not to say anything. Then, it turned into an insistence that it had come from a place of care; that the intention was to do something nice for me, like organizing a spa day. But intention doesn't erase impact. I didn't need pampering; I needed privacy. The conversation quickly became about what they meant to do, not about what it did to me. It turned into a debate over words, timing, and intention, when all that really mattered was the impact. I wasn't looking for an argument; I was looking for acknowledgment. To this day, I just wish the focus had been on how it affected me and what it meant to have my privacy taken away, rather than on defending why it happened.

Eventually, when the episode aired, the moment seemed to affect so many who watched it; people currently battling breast cancer, survivors, those who had lost someone to it, and even viewers with no direct connection at all, simply felt the weight of it. Many wrote to say how emotional it was to witness such a private moment made public. A group that also reached out were members of the LGBTQ+ community, who shared that it reminded them of what it feels like to be outed without consent; to have something deeply personal revealed before they were ready. They understood the loss of control, the shock, and the vulnerability that comes with it. That experience taught me that privacy is about control and the right to tell your story in your own time and on your own terms. This moment eventually became a storyline for the season and, unfortunately, it was stretched and revisited more than I ever wanted it to be. Separate from that ordeal, I can acknowledge that other parts of my story, the ones I chose to share on my own terms, did have a positive impact. How we shared the diagnoses with our boys, showing my surgery and the difficulty of not clearing the margins the first time, the second procedure, and how my family and I faced those challenges together resonated with viewers in a meaningful way. Those moments highlighted strength, love, and resilience which was the true intention behind why I decided to share my journey in the first place.

On Camera

In March, I found out some news about my health. I was in St. Barts having the time of my life when my doctor called me with results following a regular mammogram checkup.

I have breast cancer.

It took me a while to process it all and this is why I took a break from social media last month as many noticed. Many of you reached out to check on me and I am thankful for your caring gestures.

For now I am preparing for my upcoming surgery and then will come my treatment plan. This process is definitely intense and what I ask of you is empowerment not pity.

I will "guerdyfy" this cancer as I guerdyfy everything else in my life.

I am lucky that this breast cancer was discovered at an early stage - it is still scary of course, but I have love and support from those around me and that alone is the fuel that I need.

For those who do not get health checks regularly, I urge you to. Your life depends on it.

♥ GUERDY

GUERDY ANNOUNCING HER BREAST CANCER DIAGNOSIS, 2023
PHOTO CREDIT: JANA SCHUESSLER

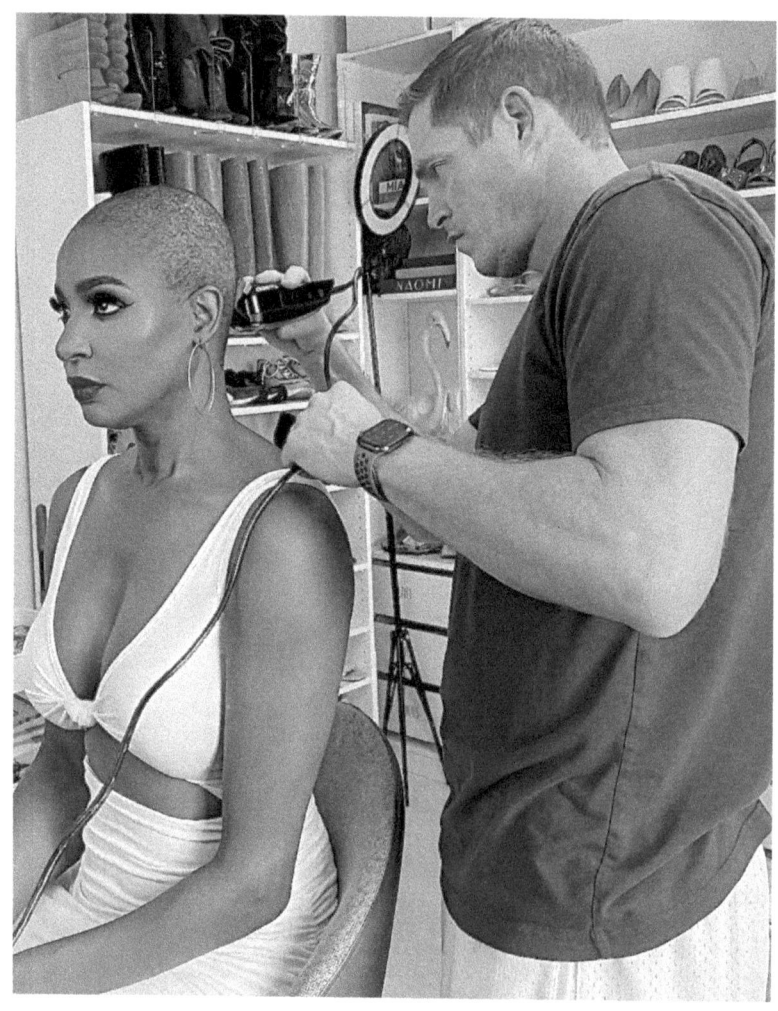

RUSSELL SHAVING GUERDY'S HAIR BEFORE CHEMO, 2023

Chapter 21

LET ME

A lot of time passed between Season 6 and the start of filming for Season 7. During that time, my body was healing. I had gone through my full treatment journey, including chemo, radiation, hysterectomy, and reconstructive surgeries. I was slowly beginning to feel better and I was really excited to get back into the rhythm of life. I felt like Angela Bassett in *How Stella Got Her Groove Back;* ready to laugh again, travel again, and enjoy being around the girls on the cast. After spending the better part of the last few years in a bubble with just my boys at home, the idea of dinners, trips, and good old-fashioned girl talk felt like the fresh start I needed. What I didn't see coming was that one of the girls in the cast, someone who had actually been a friend to me off camera, had been holding onto an issue I didn't even realize existed. To be clear, this was not the same person who had previously outed my cancer diagnosis; this was an entirely separate situation with a different castmate altogether. She was actually one of the newbies on the show, and we had instantly connected from the very beginning of the reboot. In between filming seasons, we always kept in touch, and it was no different while I was fighting my cancer battle before filming Season 7. Additionally, her spouse was also fighting cancer at the same time that I was and as a result of that connection, I genuinely believed our friendship was solid. So, when filming started again, I had no reason to expect tension. I thought we'd simply pick up where we left off. Instead, I was blindsided.

In December 2023, we had both been invited on a cruise that was divided into several back-to-back sailings. The trip was a hosted partnership in exchange for social media coverage to promote the cruise line's new vessel. Since our schedules didn't align, my husband and I joined the first leg while my castmate planned to go on the next. After my husband and I returned home from our leg of the cruise, she called me and was emotional about a personal issue involving her spouse's health. She asked if I could join her as her plus-one so she wouldn't have to go alone. Her tone made it sound serious, and she said she'd explain everything once we were onboard rather than over the phone. Even though I was already home and literally unpacking from my leg of the cruise and needed to prepare for an upcoming trip to New York just a few days later for a *Watch What Happens Live* taping; I put all that on pause and agreed to go for emotional support out of genuine concern.

When cameras picked up for Season 7 filming ten months later in September 2024, that same castmate blindsided me by bringing up the cruise as a storyline and amplifying an issue that was never really one. The so-called "issue" stemmed from a VIP dinner on the ship. As part of the cruise's celebratory schedule, she and her spouse had originally planned to attend together and were already fully accommodated for. Naturally, I assumed I'd take the place as her plus-one after being invited back on the ship. But when she told me that there was suddenly no accommodation for me at that dinner, and that I was moved to another restaurant to have dinner by myself, I mentioned it to her. There was no anger in my tone, just concern as a desire for clarity. I reminded her that I had left my family solely to be there for her and now, oddly, I would be dining alone. We never had any tension or awkwardness afterwards that I was aware of, especially since we continued checking in on each other regularly the next ten months, throughout the hiatus between Seasons 6 and 7.

During filming at a cast event, the girls in the group decided it was time for her and I to finally confront each other verbally and "hash out" the cruise situation. It was the first time I had spoken to her about it directly. This was something that could've easily been avoided if she had chosen to have a private conversation with me when she first felt a certain way about it. Instead, what I later learned was that she had been holding onto this one-sided issue about the cruise unbeknownst to me. Not only was she silently harboring her frustration, she had been discussing it with some of the other girls in our friend group. Everyone knew that she had an issue with me except me. During our exchange at this cast group event, she claimed that I had made the cruise and dinner reservation ordeal all about me, and that I had gone on the trip for publicity. To anyone with common sense, the obvious question would be, why would I come back for another leg of the same cruise to do the exact same thing I had just done? Especially when I had another major work commitment coming up in New York? By the time I finally had my first opportunity to speak for myself, most of them were already seeing the situation through her lens. Our exchange was emotionally charged and tense from the beginning. She began pointing her finger in my face repeatedly and shouting over me whenever I tried to explain my side of the story to the group. The escalation reached a boiling point, and in the chaos of the moment, she threw water from a glass in my direction, splashing me in the face in front of everyone in attendance.

It was surreal, and I felt like I was in the twilight zone. I remember feeling so alone in a room full of people. I had just started to get back on my feet; and in an instant, that light was drenched.

The water hit my face before I even processed what was happening. It was humiliating and degrading, and it triggered the same feelings I had as a nine-year-old girl, instantly reopening old wounds. At the same time, that water became a mirror showing me who I no longer needed to be. It forced me to see how much I had spent my life putting others first. I knew something had to change. There's a lot more nuance to this story, but even with that clarity, I still tried to find grace and move past the incident with this castmate a few times after it happened. That's how deeply some of those *Réjouis rules* were ingrained in me. But it wasn't until later in the season, as I continued to feel unseen and unheard, that I finally hit my breaking point right then and there at my own party. I did something the old version of me never would have done: I played the receipts in plain sight for everyone to see.

The event was an official magazine cover party honoring me as the cover girl, and hosted by *The Knot* Magazine. It happened to take place during Breast Cancer Awareness Month. That night, I also presented a check to a foundation as a simple act of paying it forward. Somehow, that gesture created confusion about the event's intent, which was never charitable in nature. It was an intimate evening with forty of my closest friends in addition to my castmates; a "Celebration of Life" event connected to my *The Knot* magazine cover and feature story.

Despite it all, exposing the truth felt good, but it didn't take away the public humiliation of that moment when I sat there drenched; especially knowing that moment would live forever on television, replayed at the drop of a stream for anyone, anywhere, anytime. It's one thing to endure pain privately; it's another to know it's immortalized on camera. Nevertheless, I did not want that moment to define how I showed up in life. I was still hurt, but the best way I knew to get through it was to keep showing up with humor and intention.

My humorous side is something viewers hadn't seen much of in the previous two seasons because of the heaviness of my story, but it had always been there. Viewers noticed how I bounced back, but truthfully, I didn't do it for them, I did it because that was the only way I knew how to move forward. And though my mindset had shifted to finally put myself first, learning balance didn't mean shutting off who I was.

Later that same season, one of my castmates was in full panic mode over signing her divorce papers. We were at dinner when she got the call that her papers needed to be signed within hours. She was overwhelmed and froze. Before I even realized it, I was in planner mode; guiding her, calming her down, and helping her find her footing. In my confessional later, I laughed about it. "Darling," I said, "this is a walk in the park compared to a groom saying no at the altar." It was my way of putting things into perspective. That's just who I am. I find calm in chaos. After more than twenty-five years of planning events and parties, that reflex had become my superpower. There's a reason *Vogue* and *Harper's Bazaar* named me one of the top planners in the world. It's what I do.

Later, after the divorce paperwork ordeal was resolved and we left the restaurant, I realized I'd completely left my jacket behind. Looking back, it wasn't about the jacket itself, it was about what it represented. I still wasn't remembering to take care of myself first.

Another time, right before our group was heading to dinner, another one of my castmates came rushing into my room with no makeup on and in a panic. We only had fifteen minutes before call time, and I was still finishing my own makeup. After first giving her five-seconds of pushback, I put down my own brush and started doing her makeup. By the time I finished, there was barely any time left for me. I threw on what I could and ran out the door as there was no time for my own finishing touches.

Those two moments showed me something important. Even after the water-toss incident and all the hurt and humiliation that followed, I still had it in me to show up for others. That part of me hadn't changed. I also learned that showing up for others shouldn't mean abandoning myself in the process. I can still pour into other people's cups, but only if I make sure mine isn't running empty. It's a balance and a daily adjustment. Some days I'll turn the volume up, some days I'll turn it down. The goal now is to stay centered in order to protect me first.

As the end of filming for Season 7 was approaching and with that new mindset, the real test came when it was time to face the reunion—the time when the cast re-hashes events from past seasons. While some expect reunions to be a big wrap-up where everyone hugs it out, apologizes, and moves forward as if all is forgiven, life doesn't always work like that. Sometimes, there isn't a bow to tie, and the timing for forgiveness doesn't align neatly with audience expectations. For me, emotions were still very raw, especially having to relive the season week by week as it aired, discovering in real time what certain cast members had said about me behind my back. Like the audience, I was seeing some of these scenes for the very first time.

By that point, I had been reflecting on Mel Robbins's "Let Them" theory. Her theory pushes the idea that peace comes from releasing control. It's about recognizing that you can't change people's choices or reactions, no matter how much logic you give them. You could explain yourself a thousand times, and still some people will hear only what confirms the version of you they've already decided to believe. When people are committed to misunderstanding you, let them. You can't heal where there's no willingness to listen. That realization, though painful, was freeing.

It meant I no longer had to carry the burden of convincing others of my truth. As sound as that idea seemed, however, Guerdy 2.0 was now fully activated and showing up at the reunion. The castmate who threw the water at me had been publicly doing press, apologizing for the water toss, and once face to face with me at the reunion, she apologized again for it. As I listened, I realized that she never once apologized for the lies; not in the press, not face to face, and she never even acknowledged the so-called issue that supposedly started all of this. The apology was limited strictly to the physical act, as if the water was the only damage done. Everything else; the misrepresentation, the narrative she built, and the ripple effect it caused, was suddenly off the table as though it never happened.

So, if I were to apply the "Let Them" theory and allow them to be selective about which wrongdoing they wanted to apologize for, in this case, just the water toss, then I came up with a theory of my own: the "Let Me" theory. Let me withhold forgiveness until it's earned. Let them rewrite their version of events, and let me rest knowing the truth doesn't need defending any longer. Let me choose what's good for me. I had already learned this lesson the hard way at the Season 6 reunion, when I chose to accept an apology from the castmate who had outed my cancer diagnosis. Even though she was still explaining her reasoning instead of taking full accountability, I went along to get along, thinking that peace was more important than being properly heard. But this time, at the Season 7 reunion, I was done settling for partial apologies or selective remorse. "Let Me" became my commitment to choosing myself with the same dedication I once gave to helping others. That is my new boundary. And boundaries don't make you cold; they make you whole.

PHOTO CREDIT: MANOLO DORESTE

EPILOGUE

It Was Always Leading Here

"It's a gift to exist. And with existence comes suffering. You can't pick and choose what parts of life to be grateful for."
— *Stephen Colbert*

When I heard this quote for the first time, it stopped me in my tracks. I thought, *damn, how true is that?* If you're going to be thankful for being alive, because you've made it through a storm like cancer, divorce, betrayal, heartbreak, loss, or other types of traumas; you can't turn around and complain about the mess that came with it. You can't say, "I'm so grateful to be alive," and then spend every day complaining about the parts of life that don't feel easy. Gratitude isn't selective. It's the whole thing, the good, the bad, and the pieces in between that make life what it is.

If you're reading this right now, I already know you came here for a reason. Maybe you wanted to understand how a girl from Port-au-Prince built a global brand, one wedding at a time. Maybe you wanted to see how someone who seemed so put together was forced to fall apart when life hit hard. Maybe you wanted to read about my breast cancer journey. Maybe you wanted to know how I found my Russell. Or maybe, like me, you're still walking through the aftermath of something, trying to recognize the person who survived it all.

Whatever brought you here, I'm talking to you directly when I say this: These *Let Me Theory* rules aren't just mine. They belong to anyone who has ever tried to hold it all together while quietly falling apart. Because we all carry something. We all wrestle with who we are, why we're here, and how to keep showing up when life will not stop testing us. It was always leading here. No matter what your circumstances have been, no matter what broke you or built you, everything has led you to this version of yourself, the one still standing, still reading, still trying.

When I talk about "trophies," I'm not referring to the kind that sit on shelves. And yes, I have those; the houses, the cars, the accolades. But those aren't the trophies that matter most to me. Trophies, to me, are choices. My biggest trophies are the choices I made to choose love and to build a life that gave me my two beautiful sons. My trophies are every time I rose instead of retreated and started again instead of stopping. The shine isn't metal. It's growth. These are the trophies no one can take from me.

Gratitude isn't about pretending the pain didn't happen. It's about recognizing that every part of it belongs to the same life you're lucky to still be living. I've noticed that people love to say, *"stop playing the victim,"* or *"you should be over that by now."* But I've learned that healing doesn't come with a timer. Taking your time doesn't mean you're stuck; it means you're actually working through your feelings, so when you finally let them go, it's real. I used to rush past my emotions just to keep moving, thinking that meant I was strong. But really, I was just doing what was best for everyone else and not myself. Now I know that real strength is giving yourself the space to process your feelings before releasing them.

Before everything shifted, my life was about emotional survival, the kind that hides behind achievement, perfection, and being everything for everyone. Afterward, it became about spiritual reconstruction, the kind that strips you down to your core and forces you to rebuild from truth. Every version of that pain had purpose. Those moments of collapse became the foundation for recognizing my real trophies. That is the story of this book. It's how trauma, when faced head-on, transforms into trophies.

So yes, there were moments when I was a victim because of a traumatic situation, but I refused to let that trauma give me a reason to stop becoming, evolving, growing, etc. The real question isn't "Were you a victim of trauma?" It's "What are you going to do about it?" For me, the answer was simple — I decided to heal my way, on my own terms. That choice became the foundation of ***The Let Me Theory.***

Mel Robbins calls hers the *Let Them Theory*. Letting others show you who they are and moving on. Mine is the other side of that mirror: *Let Me.* Let me grow. Let me evolve. Let me become. Because healing isn't about letting them go; it's about letting me grow.

THE LET ME THEORY RULES

The ***Let Me Theory*** is more than a mindset; it is a personal code I live by now. It's the permissions I give myself. And before anyone thinks I'm trying to be Miss Perfect, let me be clear. I am still human. It is about presence. I am just a person learning how to stay self-aware while still enjoying the life I fought so hard to keep.

Let Me Be
Let me stand proud in my roots, and know that my cultural mix is my magic. My accent, my rhythm, my fire, they don't need translation. I belong everywhere by belonging fully to myself.

Let me stop trying to fit into rooms that weren't built for me. I will not adjust my light to make other people more comfortable. As they say, que será, será–what will be, will be.

Let Me Be My Hero
Let me take responsibility for me. When life falls apart, no one's showing up with a cape. I learned that the hard way in that house in Miami at nine and again decades later in a chemo chair. Both times, it was me who had to pick myself up. If I can take credit for my wins, I can take accountability for my recovery too.

Let Me Express
Let me feel what I feel without apology. I've learned that crying doesn't make you weak and silence doesn't make you strong. Let me cry, scream, write, breathe; whatever clears the emotional clutter. And when it comes to my reputation, let me defend the name and the brand that I meticulously built from the ground up. I've worked too hard to let lies rewrite reality and truths.

Let Me Fail
Let me fail without folding. I used to think failure meant I wasn't good enough. Every setback was just a rehearsal for the real leap. I built a career on perfection, but life taught me more through what went wrong than what went right. Let me fail, learn, and pivot as many times as it takes.

Let Me Self-Care
Let me self-love and pour into myself the way I've poured into everyone else. Let me decompress before my body forces me to. A depleted version of me isn't the best me. Self-care is

balance, sleep, healthy food and any type of goodness that's good for your body like the fresh juices my son makes for me. Self-care is walking outside, logging off when I need quiet, and moving my body to say thank you. Like Ice Cube warned back in the '90s, check yourself before you wreck yourself.

Let Me Evolve
Let me keep growing through every version of me. Life gave me different classrooms: Haiti, France, Miami, Fisher Island, TV, and more. Each one tested me differently. Let me change without apology or fear of who doesn't understand it. I am not who I was five years ago, and that's the whole point. I'm always in a phase of becoming a newer version of myself.

Let Me Relate and Release
Let me relate to my parents' journey, sacrifices and good intentions. They did the best they could, even when their best left cracks in me. But understanding doesn't mean carrying. I can love them without reliving their pain. Let me relate to their journey and then release the resentment that came with it.

Let Me Trust
Let me loosen my grip on what I can't control. It is what it is, and it aint what it aint! I used to think control was my safety net, but healing taught me that trust is a softer kind of power. Let me trust the pauses between progress. What's meant for me won't need to be chased. Let me finally release the need to know what's next—and just live in what is.
Que será, será.
what will be, will be.

LETTER TO
THE NINE-YEAR-OLD LITTLE GUERDY

Hey you,

Be proud of your name. It will become your superpower. *You do not realize it now, but your name will mark your individuality and eventually your brand. You've had to explain it, spell it out, repeat it, and adjust in every new environment you enter. You've often felt like the odd one out, constantly adapting to help others understand you. But here's the truth: you do not need to. Just be. The right people will catch on.*

People will call you too much, too extra, too bold, too everything—all to make you question yourself. You were born this way with purpose, and you do not need to apologize for it. Do not. Confidence is not something to tone down, it's something to live into. Your energy is better spent building, healing, and moving forward.

*You will be tested in life through loss, health, betrayal, and even moments that challenge your morals—times when doing what is right may not be what is easy. Remember, you come from the strength of **1804**, a legacy of resilience, dignity, and conviction.*

There is a quote that says, "**I'd rather be a lonely lioness than a following sheep**." Keep that close. It means it is okay to walk alone if it means staying true to who you are. Stay grounded, but stay kind. Strength and softness can coexist.

This may go against your parents' teachings, but learn to put yourself first. Learn early that being selfish is not a flaw; it is how you protect your mind, your peace, and your body. You will make it through everything life throws your way, not because it is easy, but because you were built for it. Keep going. Keep glowing. #TrophyGirl

Love,
Guerdy

ACKNOWLEDGEMENTS

To My Soulmate, Russell
You've seen every version of me and stayed anyway. I love you.

To My Boys, Miles and Liam
I am nothing without you.

Pour Maman et Papa
Vos sacrifices ont été le modèle de ma force.

To My Siblings
We've shared a lifetime of lessons, laughter, and loss. Thank you for keeping our bond unbreakable no matter the distance or time.

Flo and Steve
Thank you for raising a man who loves with loyalty and leads with integrity. You welcomed me as your own and showed me the kind of family that holds steady through every season.

Our Relatives in Allapattah
Thank you for taking us in when we first arrived in America. It wasn't easy, and it wasn't perfect, but we were safe, we were

fed, and you kept us out of harm's way. For that, I'll always be grateful.

Marizeli, Shani, and Marisabel
Thank you for being part of my earliest memories and for the laughter, dreams, and adventures we've shared. No matter how much time passes or how life evolves, when we reconnect, it's as if not a single beat was ever missed. You'll always hold a special place in my heart.

Jennie
You were by my side when I first found out about my cancer in St. Barts. I'll never forget your calm, your presence, and how you helped me hold it together in that moment.

To Preston, Garcelle, Dr. Nicole, Dr. Jackie, and Laura
Thank you for your generous words of praise and support for this book. Your encouragement means more than you know.

To My Clients
Thank you for choosing me to *GUERDYFY* your momentous celebrations. Thank you for trusting my vision, embracing my standards, and allowing me to push you and myself toward excellence. Together, we have created more than events. We have created memories that will outlive us both.

To My Past Employees, Vendors and Hospitality Teams around the world
To everyone who has ever worked alongside me, whether in florals, décor, planning, catering or production over all of my 25 years in the industry, thank you. I know I wasn't the easiest, but every high standard came from wanting us all to deliver

excellence. I worked by the motto that we were only as good as our last event, and together we created moments that will be remembered forever. To my employees, I demanded perfection from you because we had to be better, faster, and stronger in every space we entered. Every detail mattered because we were representing something bigger than ourselves. You may not have understood it then, but seeing you out in the world now—leading, thriving, creating at the highest level—reminds me that it was all worth it. I'm proud of what we built together and even prouder of who you've each become.

To My Community of Friends and Supporters
You have lifted me in ways I never imagined. Your kindness, messages, and unwavering support have fueled my strength through every chapter of my journey, both on and off camera. Thank you for standing by me in moments when I felt alone. Your loyalty and love have meant more than words can say. You are absolutely part of my story.

To My Agents, Managerial Team, and Support Team
Thank you for putting up with me and this crazy life of mine. To my *G-Unit*, thanking you for helping me bring this book to life and making sure the world reads my story.

My Therapist, Magda
This book exists because of the work we did—one session, one realization, one word at a time. Thank you for guiding me through it all.

www.ingramcontent.com/pod-product-compliance
Lightning Source LLC
Chambersburg PA
CBHW050856240426
43673CB00008B/260